E-BUSINESS TO THE POWER OF

twelve

FT.com
FINANCIAL TIMES

E-BUSINESS TO THE POWER OF

twelve

the principles of **.com**petition

THOMAS POWER
MIKE WEBER
BRYAN BOSWELL

books for the
future minded An imprint of **Pearson Education**

London ■ New York ■ San Francisco ■ Toronto ■ Sydney ■ Tokyo ■ Singapore
Hong Kong ■ Cape Town ■ Madrid ■ Amsterdam ■ Munich ■ Paris ■ Milan

PEARSON EDUCATION LIMITED

Head Office:
Edinburgh Gate
Harlow CM20 2JE
Tel: +44 (0)1279 623 623
Fax: +44 (0)1279 431 059

London Office:
128 Long Acre, London WC2E 9AN
Tel: +44 (0)207 447 2000
Fax: +44 (0)207 240 5771

Website: www.business-minds.com

First published in Great Britain in 2001

ISBN 0 273 65021 1

British Library Cataloguing in Publication Data
A CIP catalogue record for this book can be obtained from the British Library

10 9 8 7 6 5 4 3 2 1
Designed by Sue Lamble Graphic Design, London
Typeset by Pantek Arts Ltd, Maidstone, Kent
Printed and bound in Great Britain by Redwood Books, Trowbridge

The Publishers' policy is to use paper manufactured from sustainable forests.

12

"If you sell sand in the desert and it starts to rain, you'd better change your business model"

Ian Clarke, creator of *Freenet*, June 2000

contents

about the authors

THOMAS POWER, Chief Knowledge Officer of The Ecademy Ltd, is a career businessman in the information technology industry, an author, educator and international speaker.

He began his involvement in the days of 8-bit computing with the Amstrad empire in the UK, learning the complexities of business from one of the acknowledged entrepreneurial masters in post-war Britain, Sir Alan Sugar. He went on to found his own company and operated it successfully, before selling it to IBM.

Over a period of years, and through numerous interviews with business leaders in Europe and the USA, he developed the concept of the 'Twelve Principles', which underlie electronic business, and which, when applied to any enterprise, provide the underpinning to shore up a company in its battle for success in its field.

These are the principles on which The Ecademy has itself been developed, and upon which some of the leading international companies now construct their planning.

MIKE WEBER first got involved with the internet in 1993 while working as the Director of Strategic Planning for a Bay Area environmental engineering firm where he helped develop a community-based online network for the freight industry.

Mike's interests lie in the relationship of a company's 'communities' to their business models and branding strategies: specifically in how technology can be used to create dynamic conversations in both the online and offline worlds.

Subsequently Mike has managed strategic partnership programmes for a Customer Relationship Management software vendor, co-founded a design studio and, most recently, became the community development consultant and spokesperson for the Ecademy in London.

BRYAN BOSWELL is an international politics and war journalist. He has worked on newspapers in South Africa, Canada and Australia. He is a former editor of The Australian. He spent a total of seven years as Washington correspondent for The Australian, part of the Murdoch group, during which time he travelled widely in Europe, the Americas, the Middle East and Asia covering Superpower summits, G7 meetings, and conflicts. He has authored other books, including a leading seller on skiing, in Australia.

about the book

IN THE WORLD OF E-BUSINESS there is no such formula as $e = mc^2$. This is still an evolutionary entity: it lives, it develops, it expands, it reproduces. It exists in an environment with other trading means and interacts with them like any other ecosystem.

The Ecademy's mission is: 'To provide the knowledge that drives e-commerce by sharing information, developing careers and uniting people'. Our core activities are focussed on four areas: e-commerce education, training, networking and career development.

This book came about to complement those activities, by providing practical examples of how successful companies have developed their own strategies and applied them to the marketplace. It is not a book of answers to every question about building an e-business. No book can ever provide all the answers.

Neither is it a statement of my personal vision. That has already been covered in part in my earlier book, *Battle of the Portals* (Thomas Power and George Jerjian, 1999). Rather, it is a distillation of the practical wisdom and experiences of people and companies deeply involved in e-business at all levels.

This book does not claim that the principles which it embraces are a total approach to e-business. Indeed, in some respects, I disagree with some of the comments made by people we interviewed and whose views are reflected here. In the field of education the views, ideas and visions of one educator or team of educators should be taken in conjunction with the ideas and theories of others, and in this case with the business schools of the world's universities and the training divisions of the great internet-related companies.

In any research, the truth resides in Nature. Nature, in this instance, is in the marketplace. What The Ecademy has done is aggregate information on all possible types of business, profession and organization that are directly involved in the internet markets. They have been split into different bins. Many of the bins shared the same qualifications, so they were grouped under what we now call 'Principles'.

For this book, George Jerjian and Thomas Power interviewed executives from 48 companies, four from each principle. That provided an overall framework within which to work. Using this framework the book addresses one of the components necessary for the completion of the e-business jigsaw, that of learning a new language. For the sake of clarity, wherever possible, the complexities of technical language have been avoided, or explained by the use of common analogies. For the executive who has remained aloof from information technology, this should provide a primer to that new language, sufficient to give a new perspective and understanding of the words and concepts with which they may be faced by the technologically educated. In turn, this is the language with which they can communicate with customers, shareholders, employees, partners, competitors and the world at large.

Economic growth is a function of connectivity or connectedness.

“economic growth is a function of connectivity or connectedness”

In the USA in 1956, during the administration of President Dwight Eisenhower, Congress passed the Highway Act. Over the next 25 years 48,000 miles of highway were constructed across the country. These highways caused both the gradual death and the gradual birth of many communities, because the growth of community and commerce is a function of being connected or linked.

Today, instead of roads, fibre optics (internet) and radio waves (mobiles/cell phones) connect us. One strand of fibre, the thickness of a hair, can provide the tarmacadam on which 40,000 telephone calls can run.

Fibre optic cables, bunched together and laid under the ground and under the ocean floor, will eventually connect every television set, personal computer or other internet-linked device. This will inevitably cause the gradual death of traditional business practice as it has existed and we will see the emergence of new businesses wedded to a non-stop, never-closed world.

All wars are said to be about economics and it is no coincidence that in this book the maxims of arguably the most authoritative figure ever to write on the principles that underlie war are used as a theme. However, could it also be that all economics is about war?

“could it be that all economics is about war?”

On the one hand, when there is no further new land to fight about, fights occur on existing land that belongs to someone else. Witness the hundreds of small wars that took place last century and continue into this one. On the other hand, when there is new land, battles ensue for domination. Witness events in history, especially the struggles of the European powers to colonize the Americas in the 18th century and the rest of the world in the 19th century. Witness the struggles of the USA to win the world by economic means in the 20th century and to colonize it in the 21st century through the power of the internet.

The internet is new land, carved out of mathematics (0s and 1s) and right now we are witnessing a land grab and a rush for the gold that the land contains. Yet however much the media suggest it resembles the California ‘gold rush’ of the mid-1850s, it would be unwise to dismiss it as vapour or a phenomenon that will vanish as the gold runs down.

A correction will come – indeed, we have already seen the start of it. But after it the internet and its electronic business proposition, like a rose garden that has been weeded and trimmed, will grow more bountiful and beautiful.

It is to this end that we at The Ecademy have targeted our sights.

This book is for those who are prepared to leave their comfortable, well-paid, secure jobs, knowing that there is little mileage left in the old economy and invest or risk their time and difference in pay to learn and grow in the new economy. It is also for the young who have nothing to forget or abandon and everything to learn and gain.

acknowledgments

WE WISH TO ACKNOWLEDGE the contribution of the following, without whom this book would not have been possible:

Tom Wheadon, Anthony Harling, Charles Johnson, Steve Gutterman, Kim Testa, Mark Edwards, Steve Bailey, Tony Fish, David Beard, Rob Wirszycz, Nicholas Brown, Ian Wilson, John Paleomylites, Mike Awford, Dave Bruce, Alan Scutt, Jim Conning, Chris Phillips, David Graham, Phil Wood, Peter Klein, David Aldridge, Matt Rushton, John Griffith, Mei Cheung, Neil Holloway, John Noakes, Andy Matson, Geoff Sutton, Jennifer Mowat, Alexis de Belloy, Neil Macehiter, Rebekah Menezes and Andy Tobin.

We also thank the others we interviewed but whose output did not make it into this book.

We would also like to thank Nicola Haydon and Sharon Ives-Rider for their hard work and timely transcription of 48 interview tapes, each taking some six hours.

Thomas Power
Mike Weber
Bryan Boswell
London, November 2000

1 war is hell

"Any person who may present this matter differently to Your Highness is a pedant, whose views will only be harmful to you. In the decisive moments of your life, in the turmoil of battle, you will some day feel that this view alone can help where help is needed most, and where a dry pedantry of figures will forsake you"

Principles of War Section I

IN 1812, BEFORE HE LEFT PRUSSIA to join the Prussian army against Napoleon, Carl von Clausewitz wrote a short essay on war, to further the education of the Crown Prince, 16-year-old Friedrich Wilhelm. He had been the Prince's military tutor for the past two years and the essay was written so the young Prince could continue to reflect on war, and its prosecution, while his teacher was away on practical business.

The *Principles of War* was the raw material for the later much developed text of *On War*, arguably the most influential book ever written on military philosophy and a standard textbook today in any military academy library. The *Principles* were written for a young student: they were not a representation of von Clausewitz' mature theory and focussed mostly on tactical issues. They were a rough guide to the main elements of an approach to the favourable resolution of conflict, based mostly on his limited experience up to that stage, and he acknowledged in them that they had been 'drawn up hastily... since a certain brevity was necessary'. He added in a note to the Crown Prince: 'These principles therefore will not so much give complete instruction to Your Royal Highness, as they will stimulate and serve as a guide for your own reflections.'[1]

The general principles contained one paragraph, which, in the context of today's e-business world, has particular value. Von Clausewitz warned his young students: 'When the likelihood of success is against us, we must not think of our undertaking as unreasonable or impossible: for it is always reasonable, if we do not know anything better to do and if we make the best use of the few means at our disposal.'

Indeed, 'making the best use of the means' at man's disposal has been at the heart of all human evolution, ever driving him in search of better means, better tactics, better materials, better and more functional tools and, over the millennia, better rules or principles.

A search for the word 'principles' on the internet using the Google search engine in June 2000 would have turned up 767,999 results and would have taken 0.26 seconds. Such is the speed of the internet: such is the breadth of the information it offers ready to be harnessed as a business asset. The internet pages refer to everything from the Peter Principles, to St Thomas Aquinas' *De Principis Naturae* (*On the Principles of Nature*); Frederick Engels' *Principles of Communism* through to the OECD Principles of Corporate Governance.

Philosophical, ethical and religious principles abound, from Jeremy Bentham's 18th century *Principles of Morals and Legislation*, to the nine Tattvas of Jainism, from Isaac Newton's *Mathematical Principles of Natural Philosophy* to Maimonides' 13 Principles, or Articles of Jewish Faith. (The very range of the information is part of the problem a company executive looking for answers on the internet will encounter – it can generate confusion by its all-encompassing search and even negate its value as a basis for specific research.)

“the business world has always been subject to principles”

The business world has always been subject to principles, many of them perhaps unwritten and even unarticulated but nevertheless present as a guide to the paths, and pitfalls, of the business process. In the e-business age principles still apply – many of them not so different from those of the past, but others requiring a different mindset and a recognition that everything evolves. In the electronic world it evolves exponentially.

In June 2000, when this chapter was written, the western business world was affected by a major evolution in global stock markets, which saw the rules changing almost moment by moment. In preceding months market valuations became based, not on production or profits, but on perceived potential, sometimes purely on the speculation of what that potential might conceivably be, one day, when and if. Companies soared to mouthwatering valuations without even having a physical existence. Launches on the stock markets came within days of a company's formation, before it had a product that could be seen or examined.

"some companies driven by media exposure into market superstar status had no foundations"

Between March and June 2000 that changed. Examination by analysts of the finances and management experience of this world demonstrated that some of the companies which had been driven by media exposure into market superstar status had no foundations: they were built on sand and it would scarcely take more than an exceptional high tide to wash them away.

In the event the markets were hit with the equivalent of a meteorological El Niño, and the prophecies of disaster became self-fulfilling.

In this world there were two very high-profile casualties on either side of the Atlantic: the fashion retailer Boo.com in London, and Generation Y webcaster Digital Entertainment Networks in Hollywood. Both could go down as the classic case study for early e-business failure as history records it.

CASE STUDY

In 1999 Swedish entrepreneurs Ernst Malmsten and Karsja Leander decided to do what had not been done before: they would establish a cutting-edge, internet-based clothing site, with physical offices in leading fashion-conscious cities in both hemispheres. They would trade across national boundaries, in multiple currencies, using what seemed like the perfect vehicle of the internet.

The concept was, as rivals later acknowledged, well ahead of its time.

Malmsten and Leander, both 29 years old, had one failed publishing venture in Sweden behind them and would later admit that when the publishing house started to struggle, and they owed people money they thought they 'should do something else with our skills'.[2]

Boo.com won the backing of high-profile investors including Italy's Benetton family, Bernard Arnault, the chairman of the luxury goods retailer LVMH, and blue-chip investors from Wall Street and the City, in London, such as JP Morgan and Goldman

Sachs. At the launch they reputedly had more than £80 million sterling in investment, the most ever given to a start-up in Europe. When it closed in late May 2000 Boo.com had debts of around £17 million. The Benetton family refused to bail it out with more money, and so did Bernard Arnault. In the event its assets were sold off at a fraction of the cost it had taken to develop them.

Boo.com's business errors were glaring, as any examination by the standards of events in the atomic world would have confirmed well in advance.

It spent 75 per cent of its outgoings on marketing, at least 50 per cent more than any other retailer would have envisaged: it bought technology wisely, but not well (reports would later say that when the company confirmed it was in bankruptcy proceedings employees found thousands of dollars worth of handheld computers which had been put into a cupboard and forgotten), and it played to image rather than substance.

Employees enjoyed first-class air travel, luxury hotels, Champagne receptions and reportedly a daily supply of free fruit and chocolates. They worked in plush offices, and, in London, from what was said to be one of the finest call centres in the capital.

CASE STUDY

Seven thousand miles or so away, across the Atlantic, Digital Entertainment Networks (DEN) was a high-profile Hollywood purveyor of internet-based entertainment. Its founders were Hollywood-based, and knew how the entertainment business worked. It could be said that, in this respect, they differed totally from the founders of Boo.com.

DEN planned to create the equivalent of a television network targeting the 18–24-year-old segment of society. Its three founders were Marc Collins-Rector, aged 38, Chad M. Shackley, 24, and Brock Pierce, an 18-year-old actor.

Their niche was what was billed as one of the most promising convergence sectors of the e-business revolution, and they believed that the internet would be a medium which would deliver fortunes to those who could provide television-style shows and visual entertainment to the high-spending Generation Y audience first.

To back up the image and demonstrate to the industry their serious business intent they hired Walt Disney television production head David A. Neuman as President, with a $1 million signing bonus, a promised $1.5 million salary and various other incentives. Other executives brought on board were former Capitol Record executive Gary M. Gersh, at a reported $600,000 and up to $1 million annual bonus, and John P. Silva, an acknowledged leader in the management of pop music groups, at the same cost. They were to run a new DEN music label.

According to a Securities and Exchange Commission filing DEN paid its Chief Marketing Officer $1 million a year in salary, and overall its top eight executives earned $5.2 million a year.

DEN began to make six-minute streaming video vignettes targeting the fastest growing segment of the US population, the 15 through 25-year-olds. Microsoft, NBC and Chase Capital Partners put money into it, to help it to a total of $60 million in initial financing, proving that financial sagacity does not lie in either size, niche or experience.

But in October 1999 Collins-Rector, Shackley and Pierce all abruptly resigned,[3] although it was claimed it had nothing to do with reports of their extravagant lifestyle, or problems with the company. On May 19, 2000, DEN called in its employees to the Hollywood offices and said it had no cash to pay them. The party was over.

Once again DEN's errors, like those of Boo were obvious in part. The extravagant lifestyle (Collins-Rector and Shackley drove matching Ferrari Testarossas and lived on the same exclusive compound in Encino, California; Pierce was paid $250,000 a year and given nearly 1 per cent of the company for advising the Chairman on what Generation Y viewers would like) was compounded by huge salaries paid, and the major outlays on six-minute segments for online delivery, against a backdrop of little income.

It was spending money at a rate unheard of even with dot coms, and it had no prominent revenues.

So, apart from extravagance, what did Boo.com and DEN have most in common?

One had no experienced leadership, the other had a theoretical abundance; one had no background in the business target area it aimed to exploit, the other was immersed in it.

> “The rules of business have not changed as dramatically as the way of conducting that business has”

Both, however, had more than adequate funding, both had enormous ambition, and both were attempting to drive into what appeared to be cutting-edge segments of the new business areas. The answer to the rhetorical question posed came, in fact, within hours of Boo.com's reported collapse from Kazem Behjay, Managing Director of one of the e-tailer's rivals, Bigsave.com. He said:

> Just because you are a dot com does not mean that any of the rules of business change. The business proposition has to be a firm one, with the right product, the right people and the right environment.[4]

The rules of business – the *principles* of business – have not changed as dramatically as the *way* of conducting that business has.

They still revolve around the basic concepts of knowledge of the market, the message to reach it, the infrastructure to sustain it, the supply chain to service it, the delivery system to ensure the customer receives what is ordered and the backup to make certain it is replaced on the store shelves, and the billing system to make certain that money comes in and goes out as it should to enable the process to start again.

One of the world's most rapidly expanding networking infrastructure companies, Exodus.net, likes to use the airport as the perfect example of practical application of the principles that underlie the world of e-business. It is an operation that continues 24 hours a day, seven days a week, 52 weeks a year, shifting focus as the sun rises in different places around the globe.

It must operate numerous systems in concert with each other: the airlines using it must build a community of loyal customers, and the airport in turn must satisfy a community of airlines. It must have a self-replenishing supply chain that cannot fail under any circumstance. It must be constantly up to date with its information, its technology, and its infrastructure. And it must rely on efficiencies delivered by entities, even countries, beyond its control. We shall return to the airport analogy later, where it enables clarity, but for the moment it is sufficient to keep it in mind.

the evolution of an idea

To a traditional businessman, e-business is a chaotic system on the surface, and e-companies appear to defy logic, and nature, in significant ways. But nature itself can appear chaotic although, of course, beneath its seeming vagaries there is inevitably a logic that man must simply work to understand.

> “e-companies appear to defy logic, and nature, in significant ways”

E-business is the same.

Beneath the surface everything that makes it work is identifiable, and able to be placed in a category. The art lies in defining those categories, and then applying them.

Since 1998, The Ecademy has been aggregating the backgrounds, and stories of businesses, professions and organizations involved in internet markets, and putting them into categories. As each category builds so it defines a space: that space can be examined for what it does, and how it does it.

Our belief is that, after aggregation of hundreds, indeed thousands of studies, everything falls into 12 categories, which in turn interact with each other to provide a framework that can guide an e-business along its chosen course.

Everything begins at the stage which Boo.com and Digital Entertainment Networks both omitted – or, if they did consider it, then proceeded to ignore. Information.

We shall come back to information at the start of the in-depth discussion of the principles but this is the common ground on which we believe both companies failed.

Information is, as it were, the cement that binds the sand and gravel for the foundations on which an e-business operation will be built. In the case of Boo and DEN it would have been a simple matter to research the situation and discover that while they were planning e-businesses which relied on the delivery of exciting, graphics-heavy content online, there was no mass audience that could receive it.

Boo was so entranced with the idea of technology for its own sake, that it either did not understand, or refused to recognize, that there were virtually no consumers in the wide world to which it was beaming who could actually make use of its site.

A few hours of research would have shown that intense graphics and video-quality delivery demand high-speed links, and that throughout Europe and much of the USA in 1999 this was all but non-existent. It was still little more than a promise from the telecommunications companies.

Indeed, by the time both companies closed, the latest research figures showed that only 1 per cent of all consumers in Europe had access to the high-speed internet links that Boo graphics demanded, and in the USA only 2 per cent of consumers in total could actually see DEN's video deliveries.[5]

In the case of Boo it was perhaps an even more important and contradictory problem. It carved its image with glossy (free) publicity in the slavering fashion magazines, eager to exploit its youthful image and its place at the forefront of the technology revolution. The publicity, rained upon Boo until it clearly believed this was its right, promoted it as catering to the trendy generation – a generation which in computer hardware terms was more attracted to the fashion statement of the iMac range than to the grey or beige of most Wintel machinery.[6]

But Boo's graphics could not be accessed at all on the Macintosh platform. It could not reach the very trendsetters it claimed to represent.

A little learning may be a dangerous thing, but, in the case of Boo and DEN, the total failure to learn anything about the technical underpinning on their target markets doomed them from the start.

behind the refusenik door

It sometimes seems to be a common assumption among old economy executives that failures such as those of Boo and DEN can be laid at the feet of entrepreneurial business ignorance, and that the solid skills that helped the retail giants emerge in the 19th and 20th centuries still apply without question.

The reality is that the internet has changed that to a significant extent.

While it may be true that in the first part of the 21st century the hype that surrounded internet retailing has become more subdued because of failures in various sectors, it is also increasingly clear that the internet as a way of doing business is here to stay. Old economy diehards will have to be re-educated to accommodate the realities of a global world where business operates in the intangible realms of cyberspace, and to recognize that just as the internet has closed some doors – making 9 to 5 opening hours irrelevant, for example – it has opened many others. But the old economy executives must be willing to look for these realities, and embrace them.

> “old economy diehards will have to be re-educated to accommodate the realities of a global world”

Few things illustrate this more than a report in late May 2000 from the market research organization Jupiter Communications on the way that the internet is influencing off-line sales.

The report targeted a new research area looking at the ways that use of the internet, rather than purchases on the internet, impact on bricks and mortar retailers. It said the results indicate that the web-impacted spending (which includes both online purchases and web-influenced off-line purchases) would exceed $235 billion in the USA in 2000, and reach more than $831 billion by 2005.

Even more important, it suggested that online users would account for 75 per cent of all expected US retail spending, both online and off-line, in 2005.

As its analyst Ken Cassar said:

> Skeptical retailers eyeing fluctuation in the financial markets and the increasing failure rates of internet companies are often blind to the most important issue – specifically the degree to which their online efforts will affect their off-line business.
>
> As consumers increase their use of the internet, the opportunity for the web to influence their online and off-line shopping behaviour grows.
>
> Simply put, business must integrate across channels.[7]

Cassar's message was that businesses which doubt the importance of the internet must re-adjust, and take a broader view of what constitutes success online, then focus on building an integrated web presence to capture, or influence, transactions which are generated online, as well as those made inside their high street stores.

An earlier Jupiter/NFO consumer survey had already discovered that more than 68 per cent of online buyers research products online, then go out to buy them at a physical store – a behaviour once attributed only to the younger generation but now clearly applicable across all age ranges.[8]

Cassar said quite bluntly: 'The retailer that does not understand the impact of the internet on his store or catalogue channels, is likely to under-invest in the internet, missing opportunities to capture incremental sales in all channels.'

This is where re-education for old economy executives becomes an imperative, and where the principles underlying the e-business message have to be understood.

> “old economy earnings-driven companies must learn how to invest in the internet in such a way that they reap its benefits, without suffering its pain”

The message, in essence, is that old economy earnings-driven companies must make the choice of staying with their comfortable revenues of today and not invest in the internet, or learn how to invest in the internet in such a way that they reap its benefits, without suffering its pain.

For some there will be no middle solution: they will have to accept that for a period there will be internet presence with declining revenues and profits, in the hope of a continued future.

Or simply no future at all.

notes

1 Principles of War Section 1, Carl von Clausewitz, translated by Hans W. Gatzke, The Military Service Publishing Company, 1942.

2 Financial Mail, London, May 21, 2000.

3 Collins-Rector and Shackley – then aged 31 and 16 – had originally founded Concentric Network Corp, an internet service provider in Bay City, Michigan. While running Concentric, Business Week later reported, Collins-Rector met a 13-year-old boy in New Jersey through a company bulletin board, and flew him to his home where, according to the lawsuit he 'used his age, his corporate position, his home, his wealth, and his maturity to commit acts of sexual abuse'. The lawsuit said the relationship continued through 1996 when Collins-Rector and Shackley moved to Beverly Hills to start DEN. Collins-Rector's lawyer denied the allegations but the matter was settled out of court. DEN said later that Collins-Rector resigned because he did not want the publicity to affect the company.

4 Financial Mail, London, May 21, 2000.

5 Interview with Phil Collerton and James Cox, Exodus.net, January 7, 2000. Founded in 1994 Exodus pioneered the internet data centre market. Today it is a leading provider of complex internet hosting for enterprises with mission critical operations. It is also a leading source of website performance monitoring through its subsidiary Service Metrics. It is a sign of the times that in mid-1999 Exodus was a $3.7 billion company: by the end of the year it was generating over $100 million a quarter in sales and growing at well over 20 per cent, and its market value had risen to $26 billion. In the fourth quarter, according to its published results, it was adding customers at the rate of six a day. CBS MarketWatch, July 9, 2000.

6 Wintel – a combination of Windows, the Microsoft operating system which in mid-2000 commanded 82 per cent of the personal desktop computer market, and Intel, the chipmaker whose chips, from the original 8086 through to the Pentium range which reached Pentium 4 in mid-2000 – was at the heart of the most popular range of personal computers, all of which developed from the open architecture pioneered by IBM in the early 1980s. The iMac, which came in a variety of colours, was the creation of rival Apple, and was the end-of-the-century incarnation of its Macintosh, a machine much loved by designers, journalists, graphics artists and designers, but which failed to reach the mainstream consumer market for a variety of reasons, among which was proprietary architecture that stopped outside developers making add-ons for the machines, and high price, coupled with a refusal for some time by Apple to introduce colour for its systems.

7 Jupiter Communications, Web-impacted retailing, May 2000.

8 Jupiter Communications.

2 the pizza principles

> "We should establish one battle order – for the whole campaign or whole war. This order will serve in all cases when there is no time for a special disposition of troops. This battle array will introduce a certain uniformity into the fighting method of the army, which will be useful and advantageous"
>
> **Principles of War** General Principles 5

THE 12 PRINCIPLES OF E-BUSINESS were devised as a framework in which an e-business can find solutions to its operation, or as von Clausewitz said to the Prince 'a battle order which will introduce a certain uniformity into the fighting method'.

They are guidelines, a railway track down which an e-business engine can travel to a pre-determined destination. Along the way there will be spur lines, or tracks to other places, or connections to other networks.

> "e-commerce is still in its infancy"

In this way, the principles are not only a guide, they also allow for the expansion of knowledge. E-commerce is still in its infancy, out of its diapers perhaps, but still at the stage where everything new is a wondrous thing, and every experience, or knowledge source adds to the understanding, and in time to the development of the informed entity.

Throughout the world educational establishments are adding e-commerce to their syllabus for business graduates: training establishments are adding it for the executives right up to CEOs, and, increasingly, governments are starting to add it to the general curriculum in the last years of grade school.

In September 2000 the Oxford, Cambridge and RSA Examination Board in the UK added it to the list of qualifications for further education colleges, schools and sixth form colleges. The Board said that it believed it was crucial that business and retail courses should incorporate the opportunity to learn about e-commerce and understand 'what many chief executives believe to be the single biggest business issue for several generations' [1]

OCR's Ron Malone said that students needed to see the broad picture of how e-business is affecting sectors such as fast moving consumer goods (fmcg), retail, financial services, recruitment, and travel, and playing an ever greater part in the business-to-business sector. The decision to introduce e-commerce courses and awards into the British public education system had been made, he said, to give young people the chance to understand the new economy 'because it is sure to play a major role in their working lives'.

By the time of this decision The Ecademy's '12 Principles of e-business' had been operational for nearly two years: in that time major companies had used them successfully for the specific purpose of developing an e-commerce strategy and product, while others found in them a 'language' with which to communicate the various aspects of delivering a product to a client.

The principles involve 12 segments or slices – hence the pizza that has become The Ecademy's logo – each covering an aspect of an e-business's development. It is not necessary to eat a pizza in a clockwise or anti-clockwise order, neither is it necessary to follow the 12 principles in a linear fashion. But at some stage in the development of an e-business someone will have to take note of the lessons of each segment, someone will have be responsible for each segment, and key executives will have to oversee or 'own' several of them at a time.

the first principle: learning

The first principle covers learning, and, in particular, learning to tap the information that is available.

The internet is a vast repository of man's learning over the millennia: a database of unimaginable proportions where almost any information that one may require is available, once one has the knowledge to tap its resources. For a business this means resources which will tell it what is happening among its rivals and allies, where and how far it can go to tap other information sectors, where it can harness online training, discover the minutiae of government regulations that apply to a global or regional trading operation: information to put it in touch with experts in the fields of internet business law, international accountancy, and the tools it may need to trench into the intricacies of customer behaviour.

Information is power – and there is no greater source of that power than the internet itself.

What is then important is how one applies the information that one obtains, because it is not just information on how e-business works, or information on what tools are needed for particular jobs.

> “information is power – and there is no greater source of that power than the Internet itself”

Information is the linking key to each of the principles – in every one knowledge of what the tools do, why they should be used, where they should be used, all come back to knowing how to get the information first. Whatever you start with, it is best to start at the very beginning.

Under our umbrella principle of learning come the research companies, the investors' venture capitalists, the information providers, the universities, and a host of other sources that at first glance may seem to have their own niches, rather than to be grabbed under one generalized heading such as 'information'.

But information covers so many fields that a book can be written, and indeed will be, on that subject alone (there are probably dozens already out there, but none as yet by The Ecademy). Some are particularly important because they lead down other roads: in particular information on legal issues, and information on sources of talent at every level. That is why in this book we have concentrated on those two aspects to the exclusion of the multitude of others.

Going to lawyers for information is the path for many an e-business, whether it be start-up or traditional business forming an e-commerce or business-to-business online unit, to a host of routes leading to venture capitalists, website creators, incubators, accountants – anything and everything that some companies will need.

“going to lawyers for information is the path for many an e-business”

Going to specialists in the talent field can tap into a global information pool, not just of people looking for new jobs, but of executives who have been there before: who have succeeded and are looking not for a job, but for the challenge that any new e-idea may turn out to be.

the second principle: planning business strategy

The second of the 12 principles covers planning a business strategy.

Choosing a route for an operation is critical. Without a plan everything can go wrong and probably will. And even if things go right, as they did for one company, which fell back on the principles long after it had implemented its successful transition to an e-business, the principles show where mistakes were made, and where the approach could have been better.

No better example exists than that of the mighty technological giant, Intel, which now admits that its leap into e-business in 1997 was ‘an act of faith’ and that, in retrospect, it started about it from the wrong end.[2]

Planning is not just a matter of developing an outline of what one wants and needs: it equally involves a decision about the partners that every company will need, for one purpose or another, along the way, whether it be for venture capital for a new entrepreneur or an established company wanting a new venture, or to provide the technology and know-how that hold up the business.

This is a principle that underlies the choice of consultancies, if any, and the ways in which a company structures its e-business development.

It also demands that some consideration be given to advertising and new media agencies as part of the marketing process, even a decision made as to whether a company needs to go to the major consultancies or can get by with in-house expertise and the help of a smaller organization which is prepared to provide an independent project manager on contract work to see the effort through.

In Chapter 4 we have concentrated on general interviews with consultancies that cover several areas. In the end any CEO of a planned e-business makes the choice, as he does in most things, for himself.

the third principle: evaluation of system software

No e-business can operate without software. Software controls its access to its customers, to its suppliers and their connection to its own operations.

Strange though it may seem, e-business is not just a matter of a website, and an internet connection – it is the way the site, the connection and all the functions of the business are integrated though the use of software designed specifically for the purpose.

> “no e-business can operate without software”

Software is the sales assistant, the delivery truck driver, and the warehouseman of the internet. Choosing the right product is as critical as choosing the right team of IT professionals to use it. Evaluation of the system software is the third of our e-business principles: and the failure of Boo to choose the right software for its purpose was a critical factor in its demise. Had it sought the advice of a systems integrator, some of its more glaring mistakes might never have happened. But this is a principle that also covers the technology which, as this book comes to publication, may well have been the mainstay of the past, but which, in the most rapidly changing business era in history, is already being looked on as obsolete.

The third principle, when originally defined, focussed in part on the promise of enterprise resource planning (ERP) software. Today some say that is a technology of the last century, and that there are better ways into the future. In any business development, as we have said, in any learning system there has to be room for a variety of opinions. That is why in Chapter 5, as well as discussing legacy system integration, we have looked at ERP from the perspective of one company which firmly believes it has had its day.

the fourth principle: networking infrastructure

But software is no good without the network infrastructure that links it through the internet to all the business sectors that it impacts.

The fourth principle covers networking infrastructure in its many forms. And given that it can be the most expensive part of any e-business development project, it is arguably also the most critical.

> “software is no good without the network infrastructure that links it through the internet to all the business sectors that it impacts”

Any would-be e-business must make certain that its infrastructure can handle not just the traffic that will exist at the start, but all the traffic that a success would generate. A lesson that even the biggest names in the e-business industry may still not yet have learned. And as we are all well aware, networking is where the average non-IT manager throws up his hands and says, ‘Leave it to the technicians.’

That is an attitude none can afford: knowledge of a network’s operation within a company is a vital element in the overall e-commerce strategy and any CEO needs to have at least an overview knowledge of what is involved with hardware such as servers, with the networking of intranets and internet, and the problems that can happen if this network breaks down, or results in delays. He or she needs to know a little about internet service providers (ISPs) and how internet access works, if only to be able to understand why a certain decision on seemingly esoteric issues such as 'bandwidth' and 'high availability' have been taken.

> “knowledge of a network's operation within a company is a vital element in the overall e-commerce strategy”

In particular, if the advice from the technicians is to go with a company which will 'host' this business information and even applications, then he needs to have an understanding of the issues of reliability, and what happens in time of 'information overload', or such unlikely events as earthquakes (which even the UK has).

This is a principle that is technical, but not one that the non-technical CEO can afford to dismiss totally, or leave blindly in the hands of others.

the fifth principle: security

Principle five covers security.

No sector of e-business has received such high profile, and such negative media attention. Whatever the truth about online fraud – a factor that must be considered – for the would-be e-business, ensuring that transactions can be made, that business details can be transferred through cyberspace, that orders can be logged and databases secured from unauthorized eyes, is of paramount importance.

So, too, is the hardly minor issue of virus infection. While the extent of damage caused by viruses such as the Love Bug that struck in May 2000 may often be exaggerated by the media, the inconvenience caused by the breakdown of a virus-struck e-mail system can hardly be over-emphasized.

An e-business must examine virus protection in concert with the various types of secure online transactions that are available, each one fitting a different purpose: it must decide on password provision, on privacy issues, and how many layers of security are needed to cater for the type of business being conducted.

“an e-business must examine virus protection in concert with the various types of secure online transactions that are available”

But this is the pop medium element of security: under the surface lie the mysteries of encryption, public key infrastructure (PKI), secure socket layer software (SSL), and all three varieties of firewalls. These are the areas that cover intrusion into a company's systems, and the secure ways in which it can transact business.

In early 1999 a research paper by Forrester Research concluded that most companies could expect to lose $1 per $1,000 transactions on the internet, in contrast to an average loss on landline-based telephone calls of $25 per $1,000, and of fraud loss on cell phones as high as $400 in $1,000.

The figures suggest that the internet is probably safer than the external environment, and certainly no different to handing over credit card details on the telephone. But the public perception is that the internet is insecure and that is why any CEO contemplating entry into the field needs to understand at least the broad outlines of the security measures available to him.

“the public perception is that the internet is insecure”

the sixth principle: payment

Principle six covers the elementary issue of payment. Payment to the business by its customers, and by the business to its suppliers.

Once upon a time this was a matter of cash or a cheque that might have been a long time in the mail. Today payment is integrated tightly into a business's operational systems – as automated as the ordering process – and it comes in a sometimes bewildering variety of forms, each supplying a different need.

An e-business must choose the process it wants to employ to receive payments from its customers, be they business customers or consumers, and how it will make payments back to its suppliers and service providers, direct and indirect. It also has to make sure the payments flow properly, and when it comes to an in-depth study of this principle there are factors such as micro-payments (the $1 and $2 sales that are too small for a credit card, for example) and a whole host of new acronyms such as SET, and BACS, all of which any CEO could be forgiven for thinking are too much IT-speak to be spared the time.

Chapter 6 looks more through the eyes of experts in the field of making payments securely and the way that in today's world payment is just part of an integrated system which links payment with inventory update, accounting considerations, and even customer analysis. It is, after all, a changing world. Not even paying is the simple thing it used to be.

the seventh principle: buying

The old joke has a trader being asked how much two and two is and getting the answer: 'Are you buying, or selling?'

Principle seven is about buying. E-procurement in the modern term, electronic relationships with suppliers if that is a preferred term, and buying tools and supply chains when one comes down to nitty-gritty.

All business is a supply chain in one way or another; and supply chain management has become a critical function in the electronic world, a long way advanced even from the electronic systems of the early 1990s, some of which are now as obsolete as the recording cylinders of Edison's day.

Companies have to ensure that all direct suppliers are linked to its website and that activities are co-ordinated so that when supplies of a product begin to run down, new ones are automatically ordered, and delivered promptly. Empty virtual shelves in virtual stores – or in an off-line store using the internet for its supply management – are no longer an option.

> “empty virtual shelves in virtual stores are no longer an option”

As the example of the giant US chain Toysrus.com showed in the 1999 holiday season, planning this effectively is not easy – and the consumer reaction to goods ordered, and not arriving because they are no longer in stock, can be damaging to the revenue report, as well as the corporate image.

An internet consumer does not look to see when shelves are getting empty: an online shopper sees only that an item is advertised for sale, and ready for delivery. Software that fulfills this function is a major factor in overall success.

As to how much two and two make, even the electronic age does not alter the answer. It is still: ‘Are you buying or selling?’

the eighth principle: supplier portals

Sears Roebuck made a fortune and built an empire on catalogue sales in the days when the USA was expanding and the rural community could not get to the city to shop. Today Sears is one of the most aggressive online retailers in the world, and its catalogue is still there – but it is in electronic as well as traditional form.

Principle eight covers what are called supplier portals – a site from which a company can buy the materials it needs in the virtual as much as in the real world. Once, in centuries gone by, the town or village market was the centre for exchange: today the marketplace has been translocated to the internet, and placed on a global basis.

And a supplier portal at its simplest level is a pre-internet Sears

Roebuck, aggregating everything into a single electronic catalogue, allowing supplies to be ordered, and paid for online and delivery arranged. But it is clearly a factor in any cost-saving exercise, curbing the reliance on phone calls, cutting the need for multiple forms and payments, reducing inventory stock and cycle times.

At its most complex it is a vast marketplace, targeting suppliers around the world for a range of manufacturers or service needers, cutting supply chain costs across the board by eliminating overlap, allowing competition among dozens if not hundreds of suppliers, shaving shipping and administration costs. It is an area that increasingly cuts across the sectors of inventory and logistics, bringing cost savings and new methods of operation in both.

And where does Sears fit into this? Unlike many of its traditional rivals it saw the light in early 2000. It is the driving force behind one of the world's biggest online retail marketplaces, in links with companies such as France's giant retailer Carrefour to pick up its supplies on the global market, cutting administration costs, saving paperwork.

But despite this, and its bricks and mortar outlets, it still sells in part through new age catalogues.

the ninth principle: inventory and logistics

Inventory and logistics is also the province of principle nine, but looking specifically at ways in which inventory no longer needed can be most efficiently redistributed.

The old saying is that everything has a price, but when it comes to obsolete stock, goods that obstinately refuse to move, or even the superseded computer in the office, the price in the traditional world may be much less than the value that could be realized.

While the in-depth cover of the ninth principle includes wider sectors of inventory reduction, for this book we have looked at those with expertise in the rapidly exploding fields of internet auctions, as a business disposal tool as well as a consumer outlet. In particular they highlight the way that online auctions have become a major tool in the disposal of obsolete or unwanted items – the new liquidator in the business market and the latest tool for any company to control its inventory.

the tenth principle: the internet as ideal selling mechanism

Kansas has a Tumbleweed Lady who sells – tumble weeds. She picks them up outside town, puts them in boxes, and through her website sells them to Bloomingdale's and upmarket stores across the world, to television studios and modelling agencies wanting props. She even sells them for wedding backgrounds.

The Tumbleweed Lady is a perfect example of the internet as the ideal selling mechanism, which lies behind principle ten. The internet salesman never sleeps. He operates around the globe, across time zones and national holiday periods, never sleeps or takes a tea break. The software that supports this must be as encompassing as it is efficient.

There are no longer working hour restrictions on selling: the internet business does not have unions to placate. But it shares with the real world the possibility – indeed probability – that something will go wrong. The difference in the e-business world is that a buyer does not have to accept excuses – another supplier is never more than a mouse click away.

> “the internet may be a salesman's dream – but it can equally be an e-company's nightmare”

The internet may be a salesman's dream – but it can equally, through the enormity of the sales opportunity, be an e-company's nightmare.

Sites must be easy to navigate (another lesson from Boo) and easy to load, the buying procedure must be simple, and there must be no delays.

Today the internet provides a host of tools that make it easier for the company to woo the customer, tools that simply do not exist in the traditional world. Some are highly contentious, others are just plain common sense. They range from tools that affect design, and authoring, through to software that builds affiliate networks, and even software that allows a customer to get a company to call him back about a sale, no matter where in the world, or in what time zone it is located.

Principle ten covers the tools that every e-company must hope will allow it to overcome these potential problems.

the eleventh principle: customer portals

Nowadays most people go shopping in a mall: it is out of the elements, air conditioned for the heat, protected from the snow, sleet, rain, or cold. In the internet age they are more likely to shop at the cyber mall – its bricks and mortar equivalent accessed from the home, and with greater range and reach.

Principle 11 covers the concept of customer portals – the supermarket through which a company sells. And while in reality the internet may be regarded by many as only another distribution channel, it is one with key differences, not least of which is community.

A community is the key to e-commerce success. Any business-to-consumer business needs, in particular, to establish an ongoing relationship with its clientele, one that will see them satisfied and returning to the site. This is not a new thing. It is the oldest retailing concept in the business, going right back to the corner store and the certainty that a satisfied customer is one who comes back, who is loyal, and remains so unless he or she has a reason to be otherwise.

Few customers, even in the internet age, shop solely on price: service is still an imperative to most and that is a lesson that has to be moved to the e-business, but in a way that accepts that this is a world where there is no face-to-face contact, no pleasant bantering across a counter, no compliments to pay on the new hairstyle, the new baby, or Mrs Pennywhistle's prize roses.

Community retention in the internet age is more than just a pleasant face and manner – although both still help. It literally means building a body of like-minded people, and serving that community what it requires. And its rewards are in more than simple return sales – the satisfied customer who comes back for more adds intrinsic value to the e-business simply through the return: this is a world where traffic is a tradable commodity.

the twelfth principle: personalization

Which leads directly to principle 12. The key issue of personalization. In its training courses The Ecademy calls principle 12 'sharing mutual information for mutual benefit'.

It sums up the reality of a changing style in the e-business world where, as in the old days, the customer is always right, but where in the new economy he or she is not only right, but is even more likely to turn his or her back on a business that does not acknowledge it.

> "the customer has become deserving of the most personal attention"

The customer has become deserving of the most personal attention.

And because of the technology it is possible to provide that attention in a way that has never been possible before. E-business is, after all, not just about sales. Indeed many e-businesses in the past have been happy to sell at razor-thin margins (some, unhappily at below cost) in order to attract 'traffic' or 'eyeballs' – the words that describe, for better or for worse, the number of visits that the site of an e-business, its shop window, gets.

In traffic lies demographic data that can be mined, and exploited, for targeted advertising, and to help drag advertisers to a site. Personalization allows an e-business to use the demographics to send content to a customer geared to what he or she has shown to be an interest, either through purchases made, or through questionnaires that have been completed,

And the degree of personalization is as great as the imagination of the e-company and its resources. No longer need a consumer pop into a store once a week to see if it has any blue ties, or pink hats: one e-mail, built from a personalization list can tell him or her when these are available, and do it without any human intervention.

> “personalization creates loyalty; loyalty creates an opportunity”

Personalization is the equivalent of the grocer behind the counter at a corner store who knows exactly what kind of cheese his customer likes, who always has the right magazines in stock, who remembers a client's lottery numbers; it is the barmaid who has the right drink on the counter before the customer gets to the bar. It is the butcher who saves the last slice of prime rib for a customer he knows cannot leave work until 5 pm but who always drops in on his way home.

Personalization creates loyalty; loyalty creates an opportunity.

masters of the art

In the following chapters some aspects of these principles are examined more closely – not by us but by confirmed experts in their fields, working in many cases for some of the most successful companies in the world, others from companies which have already built their pillar on solid foundations in the e-business sand.

The chapters are not exhaustive: in every case only one or two of the elements of a principle have been painted in, and frequently with broad brushstrokes. Those who need more detail can find it by following the first principle – seeking information. In this case no further than The Ecademy's own website.[3]

Those interviewed are masters of their art: they speak for themselves, not even necessarily their companies (in one case the interviewee has left the company for which he worked at the time of our talks) and there has been no attempt to make their words fit our principles. That they do for the most part, and that many of those whose views are given exploit the open-source principles within their own work environment, is a source of vindication, as well as pleasure.

One of our interviewees, Tom Wheadon, introduced the idea of e-business as a battlefield long before the idea became a theme – serendipitously – for this book. The world, he says, is in the middle of World War III. A war that perhaps no member of the public sees, that the media do not report, that creates no soundbites for the television cameras, but one replete with casualties, and one where domination is, as in any war, the ultimate goal. And where any new warrior needs to know what steps can be taken to ensure that he or she is on the winning side.

In the end, however, as von Clausewitz said:

> The theory and art [of war] is nothing but the result of reasonable reflection on all the possible situations encountered during a war. We should think very frequently of the most dangerous of these situations, and familiarize ourselves with them.
>
> Only thus shall we reach heroic decisions based on reason, which no critic can ever shake.

notes

1 Press statement, Oxford, Cambridge and RSA Examination Board, June 21, 2000.

2 See Chapter 3.

3 http://www.ecademy.com

3

a very sad thing: learning

"The conduct of war is, without doubt, very difficult. But the difficulty is not that erudition and great genius are necessary to understand the basic principles of warfare. These principles are within the reach of any well-organized mind which is unprejudiced and not entirely unfamiliar with the subject"

Principles of War Section IV

"Internet learning will make e-mail look like a rounding error"
John Chambers CEO Cisco

learning what to learn

FIRST PRINCIPLE

In a knowledge economy, acquiring knowledge – learning – is the key to success. Unless you physically make a tangible product, you – and your ability to absorb information, process it, and deliver it back in a package labelled 'value added' – are what you contribute to your company, its shareholders, and the economy at large. It is only by targeting and applying our learning that we are able to transform raw data into information, and information into knowledge.

But learning is no longer an academic task. There is no set curriculum to be learned by rote, containing all the successful strategies and business models. The contents of the curriculum would change at a dizzying speed, making it impossible to learn before it altered again. What we need are not lessons but maps. We need large-scale maps which give us an overview at a glance, and smaller scale ones that we can examine for detail. The landscape still changes, but the maps change with it. We don't need to know the landscape in detail, we just need to know how to read our maps.

Imagine you run a coalmine in a remote valley. You know your valley like the back of your hand, you know where all the richest seams of coal are, and how to access a market that has existed for hundreds of years. You spend your life staying on top of the minutiae of your valley.

If instead of learning about your valley, you look at a local map, you might notice another, nearby valley capable of producing more coal, more efficiently. If you had a world map, you might see a natural gas field on the other side of the globe which is able to supply the same energy at a tenth of the cost, and a fraction of the environmental damage.

If you rely on maps, rather than lessons, you can take advantage of change.

The goal of learning is to understand the e-business marketplace, and the changes it is making at every scale. If our coal producer does not take advantage of the opportunities he sees, others will, and then they will become threats. If he doesn't consult a map, he will have no idea of what these opportunities or threats are. He may improve the efficiency of his own mine, but he will be taken by surprise when the gas operator eventually steals his market. He will have to deal with the bigger picture at some stage, either by changing early to accommodate it, or by reacting against it when it takes him by surprise.

Specialization – the way of the curriculum – can be a goldmine for the very gifted, but it is more often a trap. Remember to use information that others have gathered, and to use it to assemble a broad map of your marketplace. Keep this map up to date by reading, thinking, talking, and having opinions. Mistrust people who say they have all the answers. The great opportunity of the internet age is its lack of rules. Learn to read the landscape and you will be far better prepared to judge which shortcuts will actually save you time, effort and money.

learning where to learn

There are literally tens of thousands of great sources of e-business intelligence. From online sources and print magazines to things as ephemeral as chat rooms and telephone calls to your friends at other companies.

In our own efforts to understand the e-business marketplace, the Ecademy uses a number of sources, ranging from consultancies to newspapers and magazines, from employment agencies to government bureaux, and taking in statistics from national, international, regional and industry specific sources. We use metrics from the measurement companies, research notes from market analysts, and in-house publications from the multinational companies.

Perhaps more important than any of these is the feedback from our membership. Their fears and concerns, their need for explanations, all force us continually to re-evaluate our principles.

Ideas sprout like weeds, but few establish deep roots. You should explore broadly and notice the connections between different ideas – the more connections, the deeper the roots. If the same topic starts showing up in the financial pages, the IT press and the pop magazines, pay attention. We all like to think that we do this, but we don't. Otherwise we would have bought AoL and become millionaires. Or bought a shiny little sidewalk scooter to use in the three months before they became passé.

It's a big wide world of information. Learn continuously. Learn how to learn.

summary

- learning is the key to success in the knowledge economy
- learning means making mental maps, not memorizing a curriculum
- keep your maps up to date by reading, thinking and talking – use a wide variety of sources
- look for the connections between ideas – the more connected they are, the more important they are

IT WAS OSCAR WILDE – he of many pithy phrases – who said that it is 'a very sad thing that nowadays there is so little useless information'.

Had he lived a little later in the century, information overload might easily have driven him to distraction. This is an age of information, perhaps all of it having value to someone, somewhere, but in the case of anyone venturing into the world of e-business, all too often of the variety that Wilde wanted.

The first Ecademy principle of e-business is the first principle of life: it is about learning. It is about absorbing information, collecting information, and assessing that information in a manner that harnesses not just the intellect but also the emotions.

“politics is the art of manipulating information: business is, in part, the art of being able to see through the manipulations”

Information in the 21st century surrounds us like an autumnal mist: it is inescapable. It is harder to avoid being informed than to succumb to information overload. But not all information is reliable, no matter what its source. Politics is the art of manipulating information: business is, in part, the art of being able to see through the manipulations.

And even history is no guide. As von Clausewitz told his young protégé:

> The aim of historians is rarely to present the absolute truth... they invent history instead of writing it. The detailed knowledge of a few individual engagements is more useful than the general knowledge of a great many campaigns.[1]

Neither is all information in the new world relevant to the needs of the one pursuing it. The garnering of information for the e-business campaign is the art of gathering detailed knowledge from a few sectors, which will prove more valuable than tracts of theory written with the so-called ‘broader picture’ in mind.

In the formulation of the 12 principles we accepted that information is the driver of all else: without it everything founders. In addition, the acquisition of information is an ongoing process. Like e-business itself, it is 24 hours a day, seven days a week and from global sources.

> “this is where the war starts”

This is where the war starts: the first campaign, which may seem more like a series of sorties in the initial stages but equate to the soldiers’ patrols to gather intelligence, which add their part to the overall knowledge base at the general’s command. A general in war has many sources of information: direct intelligence from agents on the ground, indirect intelligence from intercepts over radio or other communications forms, satellite photographs and many that are often forgotten. In World War II detailed analysis of news reports, and pre-war books provided the allies with much of their initial information on what the Axis was doing. Such information was used in many ways, at various stages of the campaign; much was stored in the repositories and never used at all, but all added to the background that was available should it have been needed.

In the modern world of e-business there are similarly disparate sources of information for the start-up entrepreneur, or the executive of a traditional company looking for ways to break into the cyber market, and develop an internet-based operation. There are the obvious – the search engines, the on and off-line information providers (newspapers, television, radio, or magazines, and their sites) research companies, and universities. There are the less obvious such as the e-commerce training companies, or the sites of companies in the same line of business of the one under contemplation. And there are the ones that may seem obtuse at first glance, belonging more to considerations further along in the business plan, such as taxation experts, and accountants. Even customer behaviour experts can provide information that will lead to the development of a sound internet-based operation.

None is more important than another necessarily, but some are more forgotten or ignored in the first stages. Among those are the internet-wise lawyers.

Contrary though it may seem, law applies to war, and if e-commerce is war, as Michael Dell, the direct sales entrepreneur par excellence in the technology world, has said, it is an essential component of any business. [2]

This is arguably more so with an e-business, given that anyone moving into the field is encroaching on what is essentially *terra incognita*. Consulting with lawyers who know the territory, who have explored beyond the fringes is the equivalent of a general seeking the views of military intelligence: in the end the businessman, like the general, must make the choice, but listening to the views of a lawyer first can reduce the chances of failure, and the chance of loss.

“many will go to a lawyer as a form of risk mitigation”

Many will go to a lawyer as a form of risk mitigation.

But in this battlefield on which we are newcomers, an e-learned lawyer is much more. He is not just the intelligence agent: he is the guide through the minefields, a source of introduction to the friendly forces on the other side, and aware all the time of those who are hostile to a cause. The fees one must pay him or her are the premium for such protection.

And that is why lawyers stand out so prominently in our bird's-eye view of the information battlefield, and why their counsel is so valuable at the briefing table. It is also why in this overview of the principles, lawyers were the flashlight we used to probe into the darkness and shed light on the fastest way forward for the virtual ingénue.

living la vida loca

Tom Wheadon, at the international law firm of Simmons & Simmons, is not the popular conception of a corporate lawyer. He talks of the telecommunications and internet revolution in terms of World War III. He says that 'users' are 'the ones who get their hands dirty' and those who use lawyers like him are doing it because they know it is 'a matter of protecting your arse'.

In other words, Wheadon is a realist who believes deeply in the internet and the future of e-business.

It is interesting therefore that he refers to members of his company not as partners or staff of a legal firm but as 'artistes' and their services to start-up e-businesses as 'in a sense' a marriage bureau. In the cyber world such lawyers go well beyond normal legal advice: they are information channels to many of the specific requirements an e-venture will need, to reputable and reliable sources of finance, to sound infrastructure companies, and to outlets where the untrained can be taught what they do not know.

> “lawyers in this vida loca field know that for the most part start-ups go to them out of fear”

Lawyers in this *vida loca* field know that for the most part start-ups go to them out of fear, rarely to be taught about e-business law. This is a fact of life they accept as sound, and right. If a start-up, or even an established company, going into the e-world under-funded can convince the lawyer that it makes sense for him to point them in the direction of funds then that source of funds is more likely to listen to them, because it knows the lawyer is unlikely to send it an obvious lemon. That's the way it goes. [3]

This is where the world of the lawyer mingles with the world of the consultant, cutting into what is defined as a multi-disciplinary approach (more so in the USA than in Europe at this stage, although it is only a matter of time before legal attitudes by regulators in Europe change).

In time the internet lawyer will, along with other professionals, be aggregated. The global trend is towards multi-talent e-business incubators, where consultants, law firms, or accountancy companies actively co-operate in multi-disciplinary partnerships that see their partner accountants and lawyers working together on a business.

But that does mean a competency from one covers all. As Wheadon says: 'You have to ensure you stick to what you are best at.' Internet novice businesses need input from many people, and they all have to be skilled in their particular competencies.

In time, however, multi-disciplinary operations are likely to be the prime source on information and internet start-up needs, the advisors who can lead it to a supporting infrastructure that includes the management team, the talented senior employees, a lawyer, accountant, merchant bank and a PR company. Like the goal of the internet giants, such as Yahoo! and AoL themselves, everything under one roof.

Even without the multi-disciplinary operations, the internet lawyer provides the link to the rest. And the benefit of going to him is in being shown a way to take an idea from its inception to a fully funded, fully resourced position as rapidly as possible, 'de-risking' the business opportunity.

If an internet business is fully resourced, and fully funded from day one, it is a great solution. The idea has far more chance of success than the average idea, which trickles along, and haphazardly bumps into people along the way. [4]

square pegs, round holes, pear-shaped ventures

Incredible though it may seem – especially to the CEO of an established business wanting to know more about the e-world – some hopefuls still launch into an electronic venture without having first worked out exactly where they fit in the industry scheme of things. Like hopefuls in an adult evening art class, they trot along with the watercolour of a bowl of flowers, or an evening landscape to the Tate Modern and wonder why they cannot get a showing.

They do not know if they are in the business of creating, protecting, or exploiting venture property rights over distribution networks. They do not know if they fall into the distribution element through the communications industry. All they know is that they have a great idea.

Which is why lawyers say the first step is for the e-venturer to sit down comfortably, and work out which bit of the e-business world the planned company fits into.

The next step is what most people think about first, without doing anything constructive about it – finding out if there is any money in it. How much better to tackle it the other way around – ask, where is the money at the moment? And once past the 'which' bit, face up to the 'why'.

Most people answer the question of why they want to be in a particular segment of e-business by saying 'because I am expert in it'. But being an expert in a field does not necessarily mean there is any online money or even viability in it. That does not mean there is no relevance – an internet operation can make sense as an information resource which points to an off-line money-making operation (giant multinationals in telecommunications and infrastructure manufacture do not sell their products or services directly from their sites, but they do use them to inform prospective customers and channel them through to an off-line sales channel).

But people can be experts in various ways – and not necessarily as a businessman, or a technical professional, or as someone with a particular skill in the creation of contact area. This is where the internet lawyer can assess the situation often more coldly and effectively than the clients who approach him. Then, if he is satisfied that they have themselves identified their idea, and where it fits in a business sense, he (or she, this is not a sexist approach) can provide the understanding of the market, or tell them bluntly they are repeating something that already has thousands of competitors out there. If not a lawyer can assess the project. If he decides it is a keen idea it makes it more bankable. People will lend money, give money for it.

“people can be experts in various ways”

Not until he has satisfied himself of this will a good internet lawyer pass to the first real legal issue – does the client really own that great idea?

In technical, legal terms no one owns ideas. But some people think of an idea while in the employ of someone else, and it has been sparked by the work they do for that employer. Generally speaking, that is not their property – it becomes the ownership of the employer. Other ideas come as the result of two mates talking. But what if they have fallen out and only one has gone forward with the project? Who *really* owns that idea?

Next, a lawyer will tell the novices in the business world they need to organize a business plan, even something as straightforward as identifying the key issues so they have a piece of paper to hawk around. A lawyer will advise how many fields a business plan needs to cover, and tell a client to write something down, even if it is on a scrap of paper, to cover all the points.

There are some fairly obvious things, but writing them down can save a lot of grief. Writing them down also exposes everything to the light of day. Writing them down can say whether an idea is an orchid about to burst into blossom, or just another dandelion to take to bed.

listen, do you want to know a secret? Everyone starts off thinking, 'I have a fantastic idea. I am not going to tell anyone else until they agree not to tell anyone else what the idea is. If I tell them, and they are not interested they will go and make something out of it themselves.'

> "we are not as unique as we think we are"

Unfortunately, we are not as unique as we think we are. Probably millions of people have had exactly the same thought as they watch a TV programme. That shows the power of information.

It also throws up the dilemma that occurs when a lawyer sends a client with his idea, clutching his scraps of paper or his printed business plan, to a venture capitalist who quite naturally asks, 'What is it?' Suddenly the client is afraid to answer because he fears his Grand Idea wil be stolen.

The answer is the confidentiality agreement. Confidentiality comes in between the guy with the idea, and the one he is going to disclose it to. But if they both claim to have had the same idea there will be an argument over who had it first. That is why lawyers like venture capitalists.

With venture capitalists an e-venturer is not in the same situation because the venture capitalist is not in the same business. The venture capitalist and his company are unlikely to have a business idea like the one a client brings – they are in the business of lending money, not creating other businesses.

Wherever it comes from the most important thing is to go straight for funding, even when it means giving equity away en route to it – even for the advice that points the way to it. This is yet another area where the internet lawyer comes into his own. In some cases an internet legal firm may offer its advice not for cash, but for the offer of a stake in the company that is being built. The firm just needs to be asked.

For an English e-venturer this is harder than for his American cousin. The English are no good at begging. Few Englishmen yet go into a meeting with a lawyer and say, 'Give me legal advice and I will give you equity.' It is too blunt an instrument. If an Englishman has to go and say he has a great idea, but no cash, and wants advice in return for equity in the idea, he regards this as begging in some respects. The English are not very good at it. The Americans don't care – two different cultural views.

The same applies when it comes to approaching a venture firm – some English entrants still regard that as begging, which is why an introduction from a lawyer can appear a more formal, more acceptable, route. A lawyer, moreover, knows which venture capitalists make what type of investment. Is it B2B, is it B2C? How much capital is needed? Is it £200,000 sterling or is it £200 million? Is the VC a good guy to work with, or a bad guy? – meaning maybe he wouldn't suit because he is an ogre and will look at everything the client does.[5]

“an internet legal firm may offer its advice not for cash, but for the offer of a stake in the company”

This is where the marriage bureau analogy comes in. The lawyer will match the idea to the funding source, taking into account a lot of different things, including culture.

But after funding not even an Englishman has to go begging. And the first time is the easiest. Then a lawyer will encourage a client to keep on looking, get as many interested parties as he can manage, and run two or three sources of funds at the same time.

The idea of two or three investors may seem like diluting the ownership of the original idea, but it has several advantages: not only does it provide working capital, but the very search for funds puts the entrepreneur in front of people who should know what the market will take. The entrepreneur continues to gather information – he begins to learn what is on offer, what the market thinks of the idea, how it values it – and most important, what valuation someone will give for it.

With the money tucked under the belt, the entrepreneur can then build his site, develop his business and live happily, and financially comfortable ever after, trading on a global basis and without need for further information from the legal department.

Not.

brother, can you spare a mine?

Once a business has its funding, and has set up its site, it walks into a legal minefield.

In this world, once a company has established a website it is no longer playing in a local market. Any customer can click on the website from anywhere in the world – and when he buys a service, whose law applies?

“once a business has its funding, and has set up its site, it walks into a legal minefield”

This is a problem that in 2000 the European Commission tackled amid much controversy, but it is wider than just Europe. A website can reach hundreds of countries – almost every country on earth – and address people who live in areas where there is not even a stable jurisdiction. What law applies then if there is a conflict between the person who has purchased, and the company from which an item or a service has been bought?

The choice of law and the choice of jurisdiction have always been difficult issues. Every jurisdiction has its own view. What happens when there is a breach of treaty law? There is always a provision in there for some form of arbitration, but if parties arbitrate and there is no conclusion it may remain unresolved.

Most arbitration across international borders has no enforcement status: someone may be awarded damages but the problem is forcing another party thousands of kilometres away to pay. Which is why lawyers like Wheadon remain an essential part of the information process.

“most arbitration across international borders has no enforcement status”

He advises that, as a first step, any e-business suggests to clients that they jointly identify in which jurisdiction they wish to provide goods and services, and expressly state that in a disclaimer.

And the second? ‘The second’, he adds pragmatically, ‘which is probably the best thing, is to get insurance.’

finding the man for the job

Somewhere along the way, an e-business will need to look for imported talent. Indeed the knowledge of where to find that talent can be among the most precious pools in which a new e-business, or an established corporate body, looking for outstanding e-business talent can fish.

It is also the link to another often unrecognized source of information: the corporate employment agencies.

There are many ways of encountering talent. In June 2000 Inka.net, a Boston, Massachusetts company, started taking prospects out on the *Liberty Clipper* for a sea cruise and dance night to try to spot their talent: Viant threw another harbour party, complete with fireworks and wet bar and still paid its employees $2,000 for the first recruit they brought into the company and $3,000 for the second.

But for the right start-up looking for a CEO or chief financial officers or other key executives, who have the business knowledge to drive an idea from the concept stage to the level where it makes money, few ideas beat that of hiring the services of those whose entire business is geared to finding the right man for the right job at the right time and for the right clients.

Even for them this is not an easy task. They are looking for an odd combination. They need someone who can take a company that on the day is non-existent, maybe has zero revenues, and build it into a company that in a very short space of time is going to have a billion dollars in revenue.

It takes extraordinary general management capability; these need to be great visionaries, people with a huge amount of energy and drive. People who understand what the technology can do – and what the potential of the technology is unleashing in the particular marketplace.

At the same time they have to be going into it knowing that the life span, should they err, is likely to be short, and the ending bitter. This is why the expert management employment companies in the internet sector look for people who themselves know they are looking for the challenge of living – for a time at least – on the psychological business edge.

Stage one in the process is to step back.

If an existing company approaches them with plans for an e-operation the management search firm will research, talk to the company, and to other people in the industry about what they think about the client organization.

It must understand the context of the company, because the second stage is to flush out the competencies. Until it knows the context of the company it cannot build up a framework competency model. This may sound a long way from the do-it-yourself approach that a start-up envisages going into the e-business world, where the co-founders believe they can be CEO, chairman, CTO, CIO and everything else. For many it can be the first bump on the road to reality.

But it could also be a condition of the venture capitalists promising to back them that first they seek out professional managerial talent to run the idea that once seemed so individual. This is understandable given the scathing reports after the first crop of dot com collapses in early 2000, which invariably pointed to incompetent, inexperienced management as one of the major reasons for failure.

A venture capital company putting $5 million of $10 million in a new venture will nowadays tell the founders to 'go and talk to a company such as Heidrick & Struggles'.[6]

The search firm involved in this corporate talent hunt will then talk to the entrepreneurs and simplify the approach – identify what they are trying to do and the competencies they need to achieve it. Then they will define the shape of the key people. That may sound like a tedious process, and a long one, but neither is necessarily true.

CASE STUDY

Anthony Harling at Heidrick & Struggles quotes one classic case where a partner in Germany called him on his mobile phone on a Wednesday evening. Harling was actually in Germany, however, and indeed in the same building. From the partner's office they phoned his client, who wanted a UK managing director.

Twenty-four hours later he had a proposal and on the Monday kicked off the search. Harling used the facilities of the company, pooled information with colleagues, and took details out of the company's vast database. On the Friday the German company met four potential candidates. Harling told the German executives to be pragmatic, and go for the core competencies, not for somebody who had previous experience of the internet.

'They flew that person out to Munich and he came back Sunday with a job offer in his hand, resigned his other job on Tuesday morning. That's the reality. Go for the 80 per cent fit, be pragmatic.'[7]

The search for personnel is itself an example of the way information is used in today's connected world. Time was, finding the right person would have been a retreat into the old boy's network. Today it is about an intensive search process. A search firm will break down the target market, and ask where the right person could be. What sort of company could he or she be in, or have been in?

It will try to define a number of universes where this person could be, and then break those down. Who does the search company know who knows those other companies? – former employees, people who have had contact with such a company in one way or another and are known to it.[8]

Heidrick & Struggles relies, in part, on a huge database, a culmination of knowledge accumulated over 47 years in which there is constant input because, as Harling says, 'Knowledge management is about having the knowledge and inputting it, before you can extract it.'

But that is only part of its operation: much of the way it operates is a reflection of the company 'brotherhood' or community which enables any of its partners to tap the local expertise of everyone else – a colleague in Australia helps out one in London, and vice-versa. There are always groups of people within its practice who can refer others to the right sort of places.

In fact Heidrick & Struggles' partners deliberately do not use the word database, calling it an outmoded concept in the internet era, saying instead that their information network is based on a community. And the relationship each partner has with members of that community is based on community principles. It even has a chief community officer acting as 'guardian of the community', to identify what services it should be bringing out and how the community should be set up.[9]

In an internet age nothing remains static for long. Already the marketplace is changing, and with it the search model that Heidrick used in the past to such good results. It is now being asked to act as agents for people who have some internet experience, have been through the start-up phase of taking a company from zero to pretty big and who can ask for any price ticket. They are so in demand it is no longer a question of the company vetting its candidates. They say instead: 'Don't come to me every five minutes with different opportunities. Just call me when there's something I need to be aware of, and if we have two years of silence, so be it. I only want to know about the ones that really play to my customer agenda.'

> “in an internet age nothing remains static for long”

This has had the unexpected effect of creating complications for the recruitment firms, setting a stage where they now find themselves acting almost as advocates for the industry. It comes from many months of encountering traditionalists who will not see the future of the internet, or if they see, believe it lies too far down the road to be taken into account.

Bricks and mortar companies think in bricks and mortar time.

A CEO looks at the media reports but says, 'I don't need to worry about the internet. It's not going to affect me for a couple of years.' But it has very, very serious implications, as any internet lawyer, or any internet-facing management recruitment agency will explain. And if a CEO is thinking in terms of a couple of years, he is not going to be among the happy bunnies in two years' time.

He will be gone, his company already history.

> “bricks and mortar companies think in bricks and mortar time”

and now, back to the airport Exodus.net is the company that uses the airport analogy to explain the internet to the clients that come to it for advice and help. One only has to look at London's Heathrow to understand why.

In 1998, Heathrow handled 60 million passengers. Today 90 airlines serving around 200 destinations operate 1,200 flights from its runways on a daily basis. Linked to it, Heathrow's central bus and coach station is the busiest in the UK with over 1,600 services each day to over 1,000 destinations.

This is a community in constant learning mode.

Pilots are continually learning about the flying business. Air traffic controllers, aircraft maintenance engineers, aircraft electricians, aircraft mechanics, and all personnel who are directly or indirectly involved with aircraft, training in, and on, their disciplines, are always learning to appreciate the speed of change, and to adapt with it.

So, too, are airport security personnel, sales and ticketing agents, airport marketing personnel – all in constant training to cope with moving requirements, all part of a community which is highly integrated, and where the problems of one can easily become the problems of all.

Then there are the industries that subcontract to the airport. They need to train their personnel in disciplines that range from airline and airport catering, to the lawyers, accountants, financial advisors, and air industry research analysts.

The first principle is about learning.

It is about learning all the 12 principles of e-business so that a company can cross-fertilize them with its business, in the way an airport must, to derive maximum advantage from the new economy. But it is not just the intellect that must be harnessed. The emotions come into this play as well. Information gathering, knowing who to tap for that vital piece of information or advice that leads on down the chain is the first step. It is not just information that must be absorbed, however, but the very learning experience itself.

There are no shortcuts to learning.

It will be painful, if you think it is painful. It will be fun, if you allow yourself to have fun.

Whichever, it has to be done and anyone contemplating an entry into the e-business world must accept that learning is part of the process and that the mind must be retrained on a continuing basis.

“there are no shortcuts to learning”

When he finally turned the *Principles of War* into the vast and complex book on military theory called *On War*, von Clausewitz said that knowledge must be so absorbed into the mind that it almost ceases to exist in a separate, objective way. In almost every other art or profession, he said, a man can work with truths he has learned ‘from musty books’ but which have no life or meaning for him.

> It is not like that in war. Continual change and the need to respond to it compels the commander to carry the whole intellectual apparatus of his knowledge within him. By total assimilation with his mind and life, the commander's knowledge must be transformed into a genuine capability.[10]

Total assimilation of information, which helps transform into a genuine capability. That is the e-business maxim on war.

notes

1 Principles of War Section IV, Applications of the principles in time of war.

2 BBC interview, The Money Programme, June 2000.

3 Interview with Tom Wheadon, Simmons & Simmons, London, January 2000. Simmons & Simmons is one of the largest international law firms. Established in the City of London over a century ago, the firm has expanded across the globe with offices in Paris, Brussels, Lisbon, Madrid, Milan, Rome, Abu Dhabi, Hong Kong, Shanghai, and New York. It has strong working relations with other law firms specializing in 'communication' around the world. It employs about 750 lawyers and 1,400 staff in total. Telecoms, IT and media businesses are converging and becoming global concerns. Recognizing this convergence and globalization, the firm has singled out the provision of legal services to communication businesses as one of the principal means of becoming a premier, full service, international law firm. Simmons & Simmons advises governments, regulators, and both large and small businesses. A large proportion of its lawyers have been employed in, or seconded to, industry.

4 Ditto.

5 B2B and B2C are industry shorthand for business-to-business operations, or business-to-consumer concerns.

6 Established in the USA in 1953, Heidrick & Struggles is one of the pioneers of the executive search industry. It expanded to Europe in 1968 and now has more than 70 offices and 700 partners in the world's major business centres. It is the only major executive search firm to operate a European board practice. Its international division specializes in identifying, attracting, and recruiting chief executives, boards of directors, and senior-level managers. It serves Fortune 500 companies, start-ups, universities, hospitals, family-owned businesses, and not-for-profits, among others.

7 Interview with Anthony Harling, Heidrick & Struggles, January 2000.

8 Ditto.

9 Communities are The Ecademy Principle 11 but the emphasis on them came unsolicited from Harling.

10 On War, Carl von Clausewitz, translation by Michael Howard and Peter Paret, Princeton University Press, 1976, Chapter 2, page 147.

4 a sustainable edge: planning business strategy

> "It is inevitable that a large part of the lower generals and other officers at the head of small contingents have no special knowledge of tactics, and perhaps no outstanding aptitude for the conduct of war"
>
> **Principles of War**
> Section II, Governing the Use of Troops

don't plan, just play – wrong! We are often asked 'What is the point of planning in the new economy? Things change too fast, it eats up too many of my company's resources, and besides, I have enough things to do the way I have always done them.'

Planning just isn't what most people think.

SECOND PRINCIPLE

Planning, like learning, is a process – an ongoing activity. But inside our businesses we tend to look at it as a task that our project managers insist we do at the beginning of every project. It is that document you slave over, collect your funding, and then toss aside. It is just an up-front task that produces a map, and we all know that maps, once created, cannot change. I have even been told maps limit our creativity, our vision, our ability to create new ideas – because they exist as their own 'fact' outside our world. None of this is true.

Maps and plans are only tools. They are tools that you can use to find the best route for your company or project through an evolving landscape. But change happens quickly, looking at the map and seeing where the mountains are today doesn't really tell you where they will be when they will be when you get there. New ideas and technologies thrust up new ranges, diverting the rivers of attention and money.

A friend of mine races sailboats on San Francisco Bay. The bay is generally very shallow, and has very tricky currents and swift tidal changes. He knows the map, he can make pretty good guesses as to where the wind and the fast water would be at any given time in the tidal sequence. And he won a lot of races by dropping an anchor and sitting still while everyone else worked very hard to stay ahead of each other – oblivious to the fact they were all getting further from the finish.

The best leadership you can bring to your company is to know your plan, and know how to adapt it to change. Sometimes it is better to climb the mountain, sometimes it is better to hold tight and build a sturdy raft, knowing that the river is coming to you. There are always risks, but it is always more fun to gamble when you know the odds.

You need to *engage* in planning. You have to combine it with learning, and listen to what your customers, partners and employees have to say about your strategy. You must keep them informed.

Yahoo! stock fell from a high of 250, to 60 in October 2000. It hasn't lost its map – the fall in stock price is just part of the way landscape has changed around it. Yahoo!'s strategy is longer term than the fluctuations in the stock market. Money, market cap, the personal wealth of the company's founders, all are just a handy way to keep score in a competitive game. But money and value are only loosely linked. I don't know Jeff Bezos of Amazon, but I doubt he is lamenting the $2.5 billion he personally lost in the recent 'correction' of Amazon's price. I imagine he is working on his plans.

summary

- planning is a process – not something to be done once, then forgotten
- planning and learning go hand in hand
- if you can adopt your plans to a changing environment, you can achieve your overall goals

CARL VON CLAUSEWITZ believed in planning. Not down to the very last detail because he recognized that a battle is in constant flux, and that changing tactics must immediately follow changing realities. Nevertheless, it was, as he told his protégé, necessary to have 'a certain Methodism in warfare, to take the place of art wherever the latter is absent'.

In a surreal way it was art taking over from methodism, which was at the core of the revolution in which Intel found itself in early 1997.

CASE STUDY

The business of Intel, arguably along with Microsoft the best-known technology company in the world, is business-to-business. It had, and has, almost no business-to-consumer operations: instead, over the years, it has built up a worldwide web of its own, an interlocking community of suppliers ranging from small companies in Africa doing a few million dollars' worth of business at the most, to large organizations whose transactions are in the billions.

Intel grew with Microsoft to become the heart of the Wintel platform which, to the chagrin of the Apple community, had, by the end of the last century, become the combination platform of choice in most commercial enterprises and among home users around the world.

It had on the way developed new markets, in areas where, paradoxically, many of its suppliers had absolutely no understanding of the existing electronic systems, such as electronic data interchange (EDI) and even if they had the background knowledge, did not have the money to implement a system linking them to the Intel heartland.

So in 1997 Intel, the world's leading maker of complex semiconductor products and technologies, with huge fabrication plants which cost billions of dollars each to construct, and employing cutting-edge manufacturing techniques, was still doing most of its business by telephone and fax. Thousands of orders from suppliers, distributors, and business partners worldwide essentially flowed through its switchboards.

But not everywhere – within the organization individual units had already moved onto internet technology by launching niche electronic order-handling programs.

Suddenly, Intel went from being a solitary wandering dinosaur with no e-business system at all, to a herd of gazelles where too many were racing around, never stopping to mate with each other.

It needed to do something about it, but was not sure what.

And even when it decided to do something, it did not really plan: it aimed for an end result.

It first checked out its business customer and supplier empire and immediately found that its assumption that it was dealing on a technological basis in a technological product, therefore its suppliers would be au fait with IT technology, was absolutely wrong.

In many of the emerging countries they were not. It had suppliers who knew nothing about how to use browsers; it had one who had never even switched on a desktop computer.

What it did next officials have since described as 'an act of faith'.[1]

Its executives agreed the internet was the way to integrate their operations (which was ahead of its time in the corporate world) but they decided to do it first and 'then go back and figure out how much this is saving us, where and what are the benefits'. The programme was never justified by an ROI analysis – as Intel says, at that time no one knew what the benefits would be anyway, executives just assumed there had to be a better way than the one they had.

All the company really knew was that it wanted to be in the productivity and efficiency game. It knew it had failed totally to take advantage of the time and cost savings that others were saying existed in the use of electronic communications, and that it had a tangle of incompatible e-business systems within its operation.

The way Intel applied itself to the makeover is told in Chapter 6: the reason for its introduction here is as an exemplar that no one is too big, no one is too tech savvy to learn. In the case of Intel it had the internal resources – arguably the best in the world – but it still acted like a dinosaur, and even though the result came out right in the end, it knows today it went the wrong way about it.[2]

Which only goes to prove that even dinosaurs get lucky (ask the Komodo Dragon).

you don't see it coming Popular science now insists that the dinosaurs were rendered extinct either by a major calamity such as a comet or meteor hitting the earth, or something else that delivered climate change.

Either way the weather was to blame. It didn't stay the same.

The internet for the business world is the equivalent of an approaching comet: and many major traditional companies have remained like the dinosaurs, incapable of seeing it coming.

They cannot gauge the temperature change, or the climate change around them because they are so big the information is not getting through to the brain at the right time for the brain to come back and react to the change.

> “like the dinosaurs, many companies will become extinct because their digital nervous system is not fast enough”

In an echo of what saw the dinosaurs wiped out, many companies will become extinct because their digital nervous system is not fast enough.

Some people think that analogy is wrong. They say in business company executives get to make the decisions, and the dinosaurs did not. That applies particularly to established, traditional companies with established traditional boards who also think they are in control. But that is like the brontosaurus thinking that because he is eating he is going to survive, or the tyrannosaurus saying, ‘I am choosing to hunt so I am going to survive.’

Such companies, and their executives, think they are making some kind of conscious decision and controlling their destiny by disregarding the internet. In fact, they just can’t see it coming. And if they can’t see it coming they are not planning for it.

Other companies are hedging their bets, not sure the comet will impact and the climate change, but half believing that everybody can’t be wrong. So, like Humpty Dumpty, they sit on the wall, mitigating the risk with some e-business action, to ‘keep the investors happy and make sure the share price doesn’t turn off overnight’.

But the reality is that today’s business world is about adapting to a new environment, and finding a space to exist. As Darwin said, it is not the strongest that survive but the most adaptable.

The whale is a mammal that should not exist; it should not be sustainable. It is sustainable because it has found itself a very large ocean and taught itself the trick of eating very small pieces of food, billions of them at a time. It is classic Darwin. It is about adaptability to an environment. Find an environment that nobody else is in and work out how to be smart in that environment.

It is not about being the smartest, but about seeing the change coming, and putting in place the plans to cope with it.

taking the risk out of business

There are myriad aspects to planning how to cope with a cyber future. Also an equal number of sources of advice on how to do it, much of it conflicting, much of it sometimes overwhelmingly comprehensive.

Sitting at the centre of this advice pile are the consultancy companies who have focussed their skills on the internet, the media agencies which have singled out e-business as a marketing tool to help define a company image on the web, independent contractors who can guide an organization down the way to a solution, and then leave it up and running. Planning involves the web shops that design one-stop solutions and sites. While consulting companies have depth and expertise across the spectrum, web shops will concentrate on specific retail areas such as storefronts and shopping malls: some offer modules of service, such as web hosting, hardware and software consulting, design, and graphics.

Advertising agencies, originally translocated to the internet with traditional ideas driving them, now offer sophisticated planning opportunities for marketing the company, online and off, through an ever developing medium and range of tools.

What they have in common is a place in the planning process.

Charles Johnson at PriceWaterhouseCoopers[3] works at what he calls ‘taking the risk out of e-business’, which is a little like an Olympic swimmer talking about taking the water out of the pool. He even uses the water simile himself, admitting that 'over the last 12 months, as e-business has arrived in Europe, we have seen the equivalent of people jumping into a muddy pool of water without knowing how deep it is.' And he has equally seen them suffer 'for not having planned and thought about their strategy, or why they were doing it'.

But in this particular case the element of planning that has been ignored has been one of those at the very foundations of any e-venture – that of investigating sound, secure infrastructure technology that will support the operation around the clock, provide the customer with an exciting, and attractive experience that makes them want to return, and that will run all aspects of the operation.

Leaving out preparation and planning of the system is like preparing for a 400-people banquet without making sure the kitchen has something bigger than a microwave oven, and that the nearest grocer is closer than 500 kilometres away.

That is why the global media are replete with stories of companies failing to deliver through the internet what they hoped would transpire, and had promised would be just a click away. Instead they offered bad service, bad operations day to day, and, as added injury to their corporate health, poor risk management.

> “the thing that helps build that brand and reputation is trust”

When a company launches into an e-business idea, it often goes in with the echoes of past advisors that it has to be there first, so that it can create a brand and reputation. But the first thing it must build after it has reached there, the thing that helps build that brand and reputation, is trust.

Trust is a multi-faceted subject that is built on such ingredients as privacy, sound technology, tight security, a seal or a sign of approval that this company a customer is about to do business with has integrity, and probity and such like. And the e-business has to show it can deliver and commit and manage successfully the projects that take the business, and evolve it step by step without bringing the whole thing crashing down.

It has to show it is putting in place systems and processes which are resilient, so that it has the capability, the capacity and the management tools that will prevent it having the kind of disruptions that have made so many headlines in the marketplace.

If such disruptions do occur, it has to generate the faith among its customers that it will recover very quickly and very capably.

There are many things that contribute to trust, and a lot of them require the management of the risk and its opportunities, its uncertainties, and hazards.

In the 21st century e-business and internet-provided services are starting to replace conventional businesses in a high-dependency, continuous availability role in consumer and business minds. They have already become an essential ingredient in many lives.

But to survive they have to be there all the time. They have to be needed, not just wanted.

They have to develop the mindset that recognizes that they have to be what the telecoms and power and utilities have been for a long time – high-dependency needs.

The traditional utilities have years of experience of managing a steady service and dealing with the problems of technology: they have great investments in operations management, service management, control centres and customer service centres. But what is most important as far as the public is concerned is that they tend to perform rather well.

Arguments over pricing aside, in the UK, for example, it is rare for there to be a significant loss of power supplies, except under exceptional circumstances such as violent storms that bring down the power lines across wide swathes of country. The National Grid is good at supplying almost 100 per cent availability with 100 per cent coverage, and the public trusts it to provide that coverage.

(So well does it do it that few Britons follow the example of their US cousins in weather-problem places, such as the hurricane or whirlwind belts, or the people alongside the Great Lakes who always keep generators ready to cope with power outages during the savage winter storms.)

> “with the internet, people who are pursuing the dream recognize they must get there first”

That trust does not come by accident. It comes by building up a history of good resilient delivery of its services, and when it has problems having the experience to resolve them.

With the internet, people who are pursuing the dream recognize they must get there first.

But they use the technology to convert their ideas into reality without taking the time to learn how to manage and operate that technology, or they completely overlook the fact that there is an awful lot behind the interface that is needed to make a business a success.

As the 21st century rolled past the millennium celebrations we were already beginning to get different insights into that problem and different demonstrations of how devastating to the creation of business lack of trust in an e-business could be.

Also, as many of the internet companies, the dot com e-tailers, fail to live up to the demands that the public put on them, because of their own failure to plan for demand, some traditional high street retailers are showing they can move online and make things work more efficiently. In particular, book retailers who have experience in delivering the fulfilment part of the supply cycle are actually doing relatively well with their internet businesses, because they have that experience – whereas dot com retailers jumping onto the internet without any history of fulfilment, or experience are finding such problems sometimes insurmountable.

Amazon.com is perhaps an exception. But it has been through a painful learning curve.

Trading heightens consumer expectation, and Amazon spent the last 12 months of the old century coming to terms with the realization that it was in its interest to go way beyond a customer being able to order a book in seconds. It learned the hard way that it is no good trying to sell books over the internet if you do that order and transaction in seconds but take 30 days to deliver the wrong book to the wrong address, and then bill someone, wrongly, twice.

Amazon executives went through the problem and addressed it. But as they tackled that, and as they expanded, they encountered other problems, requiring adaptability and change to meet the challenges as customer expectations changed as well.

“for those that fail the impact of not getting it right is substantial”

Nevertheless, the sign of their success came in early July 2000 when they made history by delivering 250,000 copies of the *Harry Potter and the Goblet of Fire* book successfully, with the help of Federal Express, across the USA on the first day of its publication. Such is the promise of e-business once the planning has been done.

In the beginning of this century the internet market is maturing rapidly. New and old businesses are starting to see competitive service pressures for quality of service, resilience of service, and reliability.

For those that fail the impact of not getting it right is substantial.

inside the churn

One of the first reactions of a customer online, who finds a problem with an e-business, is to go elsewhere.

Whether it be another business seeking supplies or services, or a consumer looking for goods or product, the next store, the next supplier is only a mouse click away. He or she can let the mouse do the walking.

Businesses can no longer guarantee that because a customer is on their books, he, she or it will stay there.

> “the next store, the next supplier is only a mouse click away”

The great example is that of the internet service providers (ISPs) in Britain. In the early days, when consumers paid for access through companies such as AoL, they stayed with the company. Subscription payment made AoL financially successful, economically powerful, and potentially unassailable.

Until the climate changed. Suddenly Britain was the home of free access providers: the vagaries of the telephone system meant that any start-up could offer access to the internet free, and then reap revenue from a share of the cost of the telephone calls while the user was online. Subscription-based providers were hit with the equivalent of a 600-pound gorilla called Choice.

> “subscription-based providers were hit with the equivalent of a 600-pound gorilla called Choice”

Many went out of the paid access business: AoL struggled on (although it made a flanking move and offered a free access under the Netscape name) but retaining its subscription model lost it the leadership in Britain. Freeserve, a free access ISP, overtook it within months and pushed it well down the ladder.

But, with literally hundreds of free access ISPs to choose from, British internet surfers realized they had another weapon.

If an ISP did not provide a service quickly enough, if logging on was difficult, or the interface was difficult, if any problems at all arose the user just popped into a store or a service station, or bought a magazine with a personal computer cover disk and set up an account with a new ISP.

The consumer had discovered choice: the ISPs had discovered churn – the rate at which the customer base changes as users go elsewhere.

Conventional customer churn is a topic acutely understood by providers of services such as mobile telecommunications or credit cards. They have been able to monitor it closely, and manage it. In the credit card industry a turnover rate of 18 or 19 per cent of its customers a year is understood, and it can micro-manage about 1 per cent of that churn. It is a mature customer–management relationship.

> “the consumer had discovered choice: the ISPs had discovered churn”

The credit card industry and operators have developed the ability to manage the operation, and to deliver the client service.

But the internet is different, and churns of two or three times that rate on an annual basis are not uncommon. The ability of people in the UK to move from one provider to another, one website to another, is so much greater that managing churn, and delivering customer service, is a much more important factor for the nation's ISPs. If it gets it wrong the customer churn will be enormous, and the same applies to all e-business activity.

Reliability is one of the key issues in relation to customer churn.

But for e-companies listed on the stock exchange there is also a direct relationship between the quality and resilience of an internet service and imperatives like share value.

A classic example of e-based problems is eBay, the great internet auction service, which in one week in 1999 lost its systems for 36 hours and its stock market value declined by over 20 per cent over one weekend. [4] It was not providing the credible service it was setting out to be, and on which its value was based. It happened later in a similar way in 1999 with breaches of security at prestigious UK branded sites such as Egg, Halifax, and others.

All these things conspire to the point where having that good idea, and making it happen, will not realize the incredible potential locked in it unless a company is also prepared to spend significant resources in getting it right, and being the best at integrating the fulfilment supply chain, learning and growing the operations, and developing the resilience and the service management of the business.

In Europe the tolerance that the man in the street had for the early performance failures has long since vanished. People will not accept slow performance but most websites are still catching up with that idea in consumers' minds. If these days a company is not refreshing its pages within a 10- to 20-second time limit, consumers move on.

Yet early 2000 research suggested that 70 per cent of people in the UK commerce and industry sector who launched an internet service did so without having thoroughly trialled and tested it for reliability and reaction times.[5]

“in Europe the tolerance that the man in the street had for the early performance failures has long since vanished”

What they had failed to understand is that while it is important to get to the market first with a good solution, internet-based businesses will only succeed in the long run if they get right the need to deliver excellent customer service in a very resilient end-to-end operation.

As the market matures it won't necessarily be the people who are there first who succeed, but the ones who did it best.

In the end it is not just the '*e*' that is important. It is the *business*.

all you need is a website Keniche Ohmae said that what business strategy is all about, what distinguishes it from other kinds of business planning, is 'in a word, competitive advantage'.

> Without competitors there would be no need for strategy, for the sole purpose of strategic planning is to enable the company to gain, as effectively as possible, a sustainable edge over its competitors.

Within that strategy of gaining a competitive edge, advertising and promotion always play a major part: marketing is the visible face of an aggressive business strategy.

Which brings us to Matthew Treagus and his dream.

Matthew Treagus, at AKQA, has a dream about writing a book.[6] It is a book about planning, and marketing, and advertising, and all those kinds of things and if it is ever written it will be called *All You Need is a Website*. It stems from the pain he has seen from traditional companies, some of them very large, household names even, trying to push their business model forward, and going through a 'speculative spend' in the off-line world to promote themselves, when what they need is a website.

Most of them say – no matter their size – they don't have the cash to fund it.

So he says, 'Why don't you pull the double-page spread out of the Sunday supplements that you run – that's how BMW funded their first site. They just didn't run that inside spread, and said the cost of that would let them build a website.'

That, he says, is a fine example of the 'evangelism, the belief in it'.

First, you have to go find the budget.

Big companies have deep pockets and they don't have to go about funding this and funding that like a start-up, they have got cash and can fund it themselves. They can sit back and say, 'We've got human resources, we've got smart people, we've got buying muscle, we've got cash in the bank' – and indeed they do have all these things. And with them they can create an internet business that can literally be given a brief to cherry pick or rape their core business and its brands.

But having siphoned off the budget to launch the website with the help of some of its tech-savvy employees, seeing them do well, many traditional companies taking the electronic route then decide that the City is telling them that they need to change the game. They have got to move on and be huge. 'We are going to build some infrastructure, hire some big hitters and this is serious – this is our e-commerce strategy and we are going to take it very seriously,' run the echoes from the boardroom.

Experience shows the attitude of management is then that they also look askance at their in-house operation and say 'These boys that have been with us are great, but we're going to have to buy in some management consultancy and some professional services. We are going to need a whole bunch of process, and planning.'[7]

This is absolutely right. It is the responsibility of a chairman of a large company, or a good operating officer of a large company that is going to put £30 million into something, to say there has to be control, and procedures. That's about protecting shareholder value.

But what is interesting is that they then drop out of the brave new world mode into the old mode, management consultancy, and IT systems, things they know how to buy.

They get back, as Treagus puts it 'into the business of covering their arse'.[8]

The traditional company splits by business process very well. It gets a supplier chain, sticks what it gets from suppliers in a shop and tells people about the shop. It then promotes special things in the shop. A logical operational business method.

At this level technology is a necessary evil, and it usually revolves around point-of-sale software.

People understand point-of-sale technology, and buy it off the shelf and companies can justify spending lots of money on it from ICL and IBM and that's fine. For this is technology that is an enabler, that lets the shop run the business. It is not game changing. And the realities of creating a mind shift can lead to problems when the time comes to devise a game changing e-business strategy against the guidelines established by centuries of traditional commerce and decades of theory on business development in the marketing field.

This particularly applies in the area of marketing the product: where traditionally, established companies advertise a product, and sell it, and then use technology to help handle the detail of the sale. But advertising in the off-line world does not create offers. It sells the offer. And traditional advertising and marketing agencies have one sales team to attract the customer, another to take the order, and another to fulfill it – a business process divide.

But with the web every section of the sales side can be executed in the same space, so if an organization is split by sales side, or business process, trying to gel that together does not work. What is now happening is that such problems are being forced into the boardroom for resolution, the last place they should be.

And these are the kinds of things that have to be taken into account as part of the marketing planning process.

So, too, does procurement – the web demands a review of the procurement method, with more leeway given to managers to get the technology they need in internet time, outside 'normal' working hours, and without the hindrances of traditional procurement methods, purchase orders and internal processes.

But ultimately it is the website itself that is seen and that becomes the 'face' of an e-business.

And this is where so much planning goes wrong.

A website for many boils down to a pretty face. But a great e-business-facilitating website is one where the interface (website) buttons all work and actually do things that are relevant to the trading process. The brand today is communicated not through what it looks like, but through its behaviour.

Compare this to a customer going to the physical location of a bank. The essence is not communicated by the blue logo or the words that he reads, but by the nice person behind the nice desk who deals with him, and by all the systems and functions he can see available, right there at the desk.

> “the brand today is communicated not through what it looks like, but through its behaviour”

It's the same with the web. Ninety per cent of the skill and real value in a website for e-business is developing the customer face and function.[9] And this is a complicated business. In this new world the website is the advertising department and marketing department: it sells itself. In planning for its advertising and marketing strategy an e-business has to understand that the web is not about putting retrofit ads online. It is about using advertising to provide a useful and innovative service.

It is about a service that thinks like the customer, and that is a different business to one that most traditional advertising companies are in, and where the planning considerations must allow for building in consultancy. Because, in the end, an e-business does not exist without a website.

That website is the marketplace a company thinks it has created to attract, woo, and hold its customer. A company may already think it knows about hardware and the software, but it is still going to have to build that website. Because, at the end of the day, it is the website that is being taken out there, and that is going to have to do its stuff.

preparing for battle

The Ecademy second principle is about planning, and in particular about the partners one chooses to work with in an e-business strategy.

Planning is more than a business concept. In the online world, as in the real world, it may mean bringing into the business a partnering company that has its own strategies for motivating your department managers – the 'lower generals or heads of small contingents' who understand the 'methodism' that von Clausewitz found so essential.

At its starting point it has to involve the head of IT, the finance director, the marketing director, and the operations director, although others may be needed, dependent on the type of business under construction. And the company chosen to advise them must know not just the internet and e-commerce, but take the time to understand the business, the customers, and the suppliers of the client.

Within this realm lies a host of choices, ranging as we said at the start of this chapter from consulting companies such as the Big Five, down to specialist web shops that have focussed their skills on the internet, through to the advertising and media agencies who have chosen the internet as a marketing tool, and who can help define a company's image and message on the web.

“in the world of e-business planning is the key to survival”

Whichever route a company, or an entrepreneur chooses to go down, it should only do so on the basis of consideration and planning. In the world of e-business planning is the key to survival.

Away from the world of the dinosaurs and back into the military theme: in olden days a messenger would go to the enemy's camp and offer them the chance to surrender or be swept aside by the military machine that was rolling up towards them. Meanwhile, behind it, that machine would be establishing its staging posts, building up its supply and support infrastructure, making sure it was secure with patrols and fortresses, where necessary forming alliances with other local nations to ensure they helped with supplies and did not provide an additional security risk.

The tribes that were wiped out were those that refused to see the dust cloud coming, and went on singing and dancing in the same old way, instead of calling a council to plan new strategies to deal with the threat that was facing them, or to take advantage of it. They did not have the benefit of the wisdom of Dwight D. Eisenhower, Supreme Commander of the Allied Forces in Europe at the close of World War II, and later President of the USA. For as he was wont to say:

> In preparing for battle I have always found that plans are useless.
> But planning is essential.

notes

1 Interview with Ian Wilson, Intel, January 13, 2000.

2 Ditto. Wilson says that, as it happened, Intel introduced its external systems first, linking up the outside world to itself, rather than concentrating on what it now accepts it should have done, setting the internal system right first.

3 Interview with Charles Johnson, PriceWaterhouseCoopers, December 21, 1999. PriceWaterhouseCoopers is one of the world's biggest professional services organizations, an industry household name, spread around the globe. And it is almost all-encompassing, drawing from within its 150,000 employees in 150 countries a wealth of talent that covers the world of auditing, accounting, risk management and tax advice, management, IT and human resource consulting, financial advisory services (including mergers, acquisitions, and flotations), project finance and litigation support, business process outsourcing services, and legal services through a global network of affiliated law firms. Its own website focusses on the general themes of how thinking e-business enables such a new company to anticipate customer needs, outmanoeuvre competitors, and become a leader in its markets: how acting like an e-business enables a company to find new customers and retain existing ones, strengthen relations with partners and deliver goods and services efficiently, and how becoming an e-business involves transforming a company into an agile, information age corporation.

4 eBay was down several times in 1999 for a variety of technical reasons, some of them never publicly explained. In the major stoppage it recompensed some of its sellers, and extended auction times and the whole episode of coping with customer ire, and tracking down the problem resulted in a charge on its revenues of several million dollars.

5 AKQA is one of Britain's leading e-services companies. It understands the combined power of advertising and the internet, and what this combination can deliver to e-business clients and consumers. Like many other companies in this arena it partners with suppliers to deliver a more seamless service. It has a blue-chip client list, operates from architect-designed offices in Central London's Jermyn Street and is a prime example of the subject it preaches – an entrepreneurial vision that has achieved success on its own merits. It was founded by Ajaz Ahmed, Matthew Treagus, Dan Norris-Jones, and James Hilton, who brought together a combination of unique disciplines from business to technology and the creativity that equates to von Clausewitz' inescapable art.

6 Interview with Matthew Treagus, Chief Operating Officer of AKQA, November 26, 1999.

7 Ditto.

8 Ditto.

9 Ditto. According to a report of June 12, 2000 by CreativeGood, a consulting firm in New York, e-merchants in the USA could save themselves $20 billion sales a year by improving their website design, navigation, and overall ease of use. It said that many sites paid little attention to what visitors did once they got there, and merchants typically failed their customers on page design, site search, and the checkout process. It criticized high-profile Marthastewart.com for letting customers add out-of-stock items to the shopping cart without telling them until they reached the final checkout that the items were unavailable. It said others failed to label products at all, or if they did so did it badly; they tried to pack too much information onto a page, and many required customers to fill out a lengthy questionnaire before they could actually browse for goods. In short, it said, e-commerce sites might be interesting to look at but were not easy for many customers to use. H. Robert Wientzen, president of the Direct Marketing Association said this might be because e-tailers are still trying to shed their high-tech habits, and reverence for technology.

5 electricity can kill you: evaluation of system software

> "The first and most important rule to observe in order to accomplish these purposes is to use our entire forces with the utmost energy. Any moderation would leave us short of our aim. Even with everything in our favor we should be unwise not to make the greatest effort in order to make the result perfectly certain. For such effort can never produce negative results. The greater the effort, the sooner the suffering will cease"
>
> **Principles of War** Section III, Strategy

technology is a fickle friend You have seen the light. You want to revamp your business, and you are ready to start preparing your board for a 'cultural transition' into the new economy. You have a vision for the new office: paperless, bright, colourful, and filled with happy, teenage web wizards, drinking espresso and 'creating value'.

Great. But what do you have now? When you start to talk to people at all different levels of a company, you begin to discover how little information about the technology infrastructure trickles up to the higher echelons. Even chief information officers are no longer technical, they prefer strategy, and are content to leave the details to the kids in the basement.

Our experience is that most companies – even very technical ones – have very little idea of what they already process. This is true in terms of software, internal technical resources, automated business systems, and – most crucially – databases. To tackle the third principle, evaluation of system software, you are going to have to let the technicians teach you a bit about what you already have.

THIRD PRINCIPLE

It helps to have a little understanding of how software sales work and where software companies make their money. Software companies sell 'solutions', which may be simple accounting packages, or fully integrated enterprise resource planning (ERP) applications. Their real profit, however, comes not from licence fees, but from ongoing training, support and maintenance contracts, which usually cost between 10 and 20 per cent of the up-front licence cost per year.

By locking you into maintenance and training agreements, software companies can foist on you new products and services that may have very little to do with your business plans. Software companies are very good at selling 'vision' and 'futures', but the whole thing is really about data – your data – being processed.

To avoid this, you need to get a list of what you have and check it twice. You have to find out what each package does, why you have it, and whether you still need it. For each item on your list, ask yourself: does it fit the plan? There should be nothing on your list that your technical staff can't teach you in a few days. When you don't understand what they are talking about, do not assume it is because you are not clever enough. Very few of the software salespeople who got your company to part with its cash are technical either.

questions to ask

Where your technical people are going through everything, there are a few questions you should constantly bear in mind. These are:

- where is all you company's information actually stored?
- who can access it?
- what do all the different systems do?
- why were they purchased?
- did they actually provide the solution they were bought?
- has anyone looked at the return on investment since the sales team's initial presentation?
- if so, does it match the team's forcast?
- are your systems compatible with one another?
- are you spending money on making systems work together when they don't need to?
- are you hanging on to legacy systems that should be discarded?

In short, you cannot march succesfully into the future without a full understanding of the past. It is our experience that technology, just by being a bit intimidating, has a remarkable way of erasing its own past. You need to focus on the future, but learn from the past. You will be surprised to find out how many of the solultions you were sold are actually being used for entirely different purposes. This is all information that will be very usefull in filling in the map that you are making.

summary

- it is vital that you know and understand the systems you already have
- make a list of all the systems you have, and get your technical staff to explain everything about them
- ask the questions above of every system in your company

technology delivers The idea is the beginning: the technology is the way of delivering the idea. It goes almost without saying therefore that the technology must be capable of such delivery, seamlessly, effortlessly, and with all contingencies taken into account – the evaluation of system software.

“the idea is the beginning: the technology is the way of delivering the idea”

There is a joke by comedian Dave Barry that has made its way into some compilations of quotations, the kind that try to avoid Plutarch, Shakespeare, and the Bible:

Plumbing is one of the easier do-it-yourself activities, requiring only a few simple tools and a willingness to stick your own arm into a clogged toilet. In fact, you can solve many home plumbing problems, such as an annoying faucet drip, merely by turning up the radio.

But before we get into specific techniques let us look at how plumbing works. A plumbing system is very much like your electrical system, except that instead of electricity it has water and instead of wires it has pipes, and instead of radios and waffle irons it has faucets and toilets.

So the truth is that your plumbing system is nothing like your electrical system, which is good because electricity can kill you.

software glue

Plumbing in the e-business world is the technology system and that means the software: getting it right means the faucets and the toilets work properly. Getting it wrong turns it into a faulty electrical system. And, as the man said, electricity can kill you.

So unless a company wants to risk a major shock it has to look carefully at the software that will underpin its e-business, before it goes out and buys it and discovers it will not do the whole job. It means evaluating what is new in software – and new technology is emerging all the time – and how it works with, or improves upon any of the legacy software a company may have, or how it integrates with it if a company needs to keep the system it has built up over time.

Software is about gluing the company together.

The history of e-business is already littered with instances where even the most prestigious companies failed to recognize the demands that could be made upon the software systems that underpinned their business, and the penalties that followed their failure.

“software is about gluing the company together”

In the case of Boo.com the technology became the consuming vision: overwhelming the business intent instead of aiding it. But Boo.com was a new business, whose founders had only failure behind them. How much more indicative of the problem is the prestigious Encyclopaedia Britannica, the font of knowledge around the world for more than 100 years?

When it went online it failed to use its own strengths – research, education – to investigate the demands that would be placed upon its systems, and for more than a month after its debut in 1999 as a free offering its site was inaccessible. Too much unexpected demand on both the hardware and the software swamped the knowledge source (see Chapter 6).

CASE STUDY

The same problems have affected traditional business moving online, and established on-line business – the case of Toysrus.com is a clear example. It failed to make the impact of its off-line parent in 1998, and decided to pour more resources into its operation in 1999. Two CEOs later in the year it believed it finally had everything in place, administratively and technologically – and it launched, just before the Thanksgiving holiday season, a special offer.

Before Christmas its system was overloaded, it was handing out $100 rebates and its image had suffered yet again. It failed to evaluate the demands that would be made upon it, not just on the visible face of the website but on the underlying integrated systems, the networks of muscles that gives any e-enterprise its strength and its advantages – and its vulnerabilities.

The airport analogy from Exodus.net is worth revisiting here.

Every day the airport uses computers to control its network of operations, from the passenger ticketing systems, through to the control tower; from the water and power supplies through to the elevators and escalators, and the docking systems for the aircraft.

The technology handles the integrated public transport system, the medical centres, the shops, the baggage reclaims, the lost property offices, the cafes and bars. Immigration and police, the training sector, and the cargo services use it. Purchasing and warehousing of direct goods flows through technology, it controls the delivery of provisions to stores and planes, and trash removal from the myriad outlets including the arriving aircraft.

At Heathrow, London, £1 million is invested every day in facilities and customer service development. The rail link that connects the airport to Central London cost £450 million alone. Investment in redeveloping terminals is over £90 million and the developments never stop. At Heathrow all this deployment took months of evaluating the software systems which drive the technology that in turn provides the efficiencies and the functionality that are the face of the operations.

For a budding e-business that process begins not at the computer store, or at the consultancy, or in the pages of a product magazine – but with whatever may already exist to support a business.

In the case of a start-up this stage may not apply, but for most companies, even one- or two-man operations, there are existing systems which have been used for some time and have a value and a worth, and moreover data which need to be retained.

> “software enables and controls the link between company information and its internet site(s)”

The current software infrastructure system has to be evaluated, and a decision made on what can be kept, consolidated and integrated and what must be abandoned. It is critical to bring everything together internally before making an attack on the online world. Software enables and controls the link between company information and its internet site(s). Any company going into electronic operations has to understand that link and recognize why it is no longer necessary to regard the website and company information as separate systems.

ERP is dead; long live ERP!

The enormity of the operation for an existing company should become clear with only a moment's thought: for a company with enterprise resource planning (ERP) systems already in place, it will involve the whole of the ERP system and integration of many complicated parts of the company, such as sales, personnel and finance, which need to continue as fully functioning entities while the overhaul is ongoing.

This is where many traditional company executives start to look askance at some aspects of the internet cutting edge. For there is a train of thought that says that ERP, the backbone of so many traditional companies in the past 30 years, has had its day.

It is a feeling that has had an acute effect on Europe's largest software producer, SAP, whose success is rooted in the ERP sector but which, for the past year, has been struggling to keep it alive, while it sought new channels more exploitable in an e-business world.

Indeed, some industry leaders openly say that ERP vendors are failing the industry, and that this is a technology that will never lend itself to the internet.[1]

This is not to say that everyone believes ERP is dead. Just that it is being seen as increasingly difficult to bring into the same environment as e-business. ERP is at the back office side of the business. It is trying to push forward into the enterprise, but its focus is in terms of supply chains – and now there are lots of customer relation management (CRM) vendors coming in and targeting that.

“in this complex world companies that advise on system integration sit at the centre”

What a company must do is integrate these things within the enterprise, and externally. It has to glue an enterprise together and give it a seamless, focussed electronic delivery. In this complex world companies that advise on system integration sit at the centre. They look at the islands of systems and data in an established, traditional company and pull them together and co-ordinate them effectively to give customers a seamless electronic business vision. The imperative is that they focus it most from the customers' perspective.

Whatever their future, ERP systems are known and well regarded for their effectiveness in supply chain management. That is their priority. They deal in efficiency. Procuring goods, reducing the costs, moving the process of delivering and producing and on the whole aimed at manufacturers and distributors primarily. That is a very important element.

CRM is aimed at more effectively supporting the sales and marketing efficiencies of a business's customers, turning to one-to-one marketing initiatives with customers and getting more efficient cross-selling.

Traditional companies which have both say, 'Right, CRM is focussed on the selling chain, ERP is focussed on the supply chain. So what else?'

As we said, both are important elements of the system. But the mistake these companies make is not ensuring that they come together to ensure a seamless flow the whole way through. Today's world is all about integrated electronic business. Transactions inside the enterprise and external to the enterprise. A company eyeing the internet must first examine what it already does, then what it thinks it is going to do, in terms of e-business; where it is trying to go with the electronic business initiatives, where it believes its marketplace to be, and then validate what the market is.

Then it must decide which existing systems are worth keeping. Validate them, decide if the business features within those systems support what the client is trying to do as an electronic business, then make decisions on whether certain parts and certain systems must be replaced, or changed.

The focus should be on how to get the best business advantage as early as possible, and then follow through with the rollout of increments that add business value each time. No one can afford to wait too long to bring forward an electronic business vision.

“no one can afford to wait too long to bring forward an electronic business vision”

And while revolution is the method that seems golden for some, evolution is how the majority will get there and ensure that there is business value being driven out.

calling in the plumber

In this business of getting the software to flow properly around the circuit, there is a time to call in the plumber.

Clearly, one of the most critical things is getting the right foundation for electronic business into an organization. This means the key executives of companies, and in particular the head of IT, or sales and marketing directors whose responsibility this is, must have a general understanding of how the system will work, and what software will drive it. But sometimes the advising on it, and the implementation of it is best left in the hands of the specialized system integration companies – the plumbers of the internet world.

“a company will not survive as an electronic business if it is out of action”

For them the problems start right from the first contact with a client. A percentage of customers who go to a systems integrator will have accepted already that they need to do something about electronic business, but will readily admit they are not clear what they should do, what the priorities are, and how much they have to move online. Others have a clear business vision about what they want to achieve.

Some will assist the plumber in building an idea of what the business vision is, and then defining the sort of infrastructure they need to put in place to give them flexibility to move forward.

Others will know they only need help on the enabling technology, to give them building blocks, and then for the plumber to come back and weld everything together.

At the very top of their demand list, when the plumber comes to call, is a system which is absolutely secure, and which underpins a company 24 hours a day, seven days a week, 52 weeks a year, with high and unpredictable volumes. As part of that it has to put away the crystal ball and say that this must also be a system that can be scaled upwards easily.

A company will not survive as an electronic business if it is out of action. It will not attract a lost deal, or a lost customer back. Which means that it needs high availability, quick response times, and basically to be able to get the systems on the software it is using – because that is all it has got.

High availability is another industry buzzword that may need some explaining. Look at it this way – if somebody gives you a share tip and you use Barclays Stockbrokers you want to be assured that when you actually go in to make that transaction, the service is going to be available. Because if it isn't, or if you have to go back half an hour later, or you phone the stockbroker and get the 'thank you for phoning Barclays Stockbrokers… if you have a touch phone hit etc.', by the time you are through half an hour has passed and the price of that stock has gone up by 20 per cent. You have missed the boat.

You want to be sure when you get onto Barclays Stockbrokers, or Datex, or E*Trade or whoever you want to think of, that when you hit the button you are going to buy that stock at $26 and you are not going to have to buy it for $30 in half an hour's time.

That in a nutshell is high availability.

No software vendor can yet give a guarantee on response time from the software because too many outside factors come into play. But every business can get a high-availability, high-transaction, high-volume engine that allows it, with hard work and the rest of the design, to offer something close to it. [2]

notes

1 Erwin Koenig, former physicist and now CEO of Software AG has been an outspoken critic of ERP in the internet world. Based in Darmstadt, Germany, today, 30 years after its creation, Software AG is one of the largest system software companies in the world. It is represented in more than 60 countries by subsidiaries or partners, and its products are used in more than 90 countries. It was also, at one stage, a giant with problems, and an example of a company that saw the coming of the internet and adapted to accommodate, then embrace it. In 1996 there was a realization – which came on top of a £6 million loss – that the company was not exploiting the internet. It had, in the words of company executives, lost direction and run out of steam. That is when Koenig and two others came onboard: they cut 20 per cent of the staff worldwide, abandoned non-

strategic ventures such as applications development and selling and running the products: they sold the rights in products in the USA to another organization to raise money – and then they went on a rebuilding the company mission, to position it for the internet age. It meant re-engineering, refocussing and essentially, retraining everybody.

Koenig said later: 'We didn't have to go down the electronic commerce route. We could have gone another way and grown the business in other areas. But we clearly saw that this is where the major payback is, and that is why we chose this route.'

And this became not just its story, but also its business.

2 Interview with Mark Edwards and Steve Bailey, Software AG, December 2, 1999.

6 three kinds of death: networking infrastructure

> “The aggressor ... must usually gather his forces from a distance and therefore with great difficulty. Lest he find himself short of effectives, he must organize the recruiting of troops and the transport of arms a long time before they are needed. The roads of our lines of operation must be covered constantly with transports of soldiers and suppliers”
>
> **Principles of War** Offensive Principles 3

a miniature economy

Software systems and databases are linked together by a communication infrastructure to create a network. Networks are powerful when they are simple. (Simple to understand and use, that is. They are bit trickier to actually build and keep working!)

Data is the raw material, databases are the warehouses in which it is stored, and software applications are the factories that make something valuable – usable information – from the raw material. The network is the infrastructure which connects raw material, warehouses and factories, and allows the finished product to get to the consumers. The consumers being you, your customers, your partners, and your suppliers. Simple.

FOURTH PRINCIPLE

The trick is to exploit what you learned from examining your systems (the third principle). Once you understand what you have, you can decide whether the new data will be more valuable shared within the company, outside the company, or with the competition. You should then find out whether your communications network allows you to share what you want with whom you want.

the hidden cost of bad communication

The web's promise is instant communication, with no need to store multiple databases. It offers easily accessible information to whomever needs it to create value for the company.

And that is where the focus gets lost: creating value.

The transportation industry is very efficient at distributing goods and merchandise all over the world. The jacket you buy in the shopping mall may have been assembled in India from Indonesian fabric and South American buttons, but each of those components will have been handled as few times as possible, because each time it is handled there is a charge.

We understand that in the physical world, but we don't apply it to technology because we imagine that there are no handling charges – or transaction costs – on internet traffic. It isn't true. Every piece of information you put up on your website or intranet is using people's time. They read it, print it, file it away.

For those of you who rely on e-mail as your primary communication tool: has it become a burden yet? Do you dread the hours of reading and responding to other people's self-protecting, 'informational' e-mail that has little to do with your job?

You need to bear in mind these hidden transaction costs – all the time everyone spends filtering out all the useless information they receive. If you apply that thinking to all your communications – both on and off line – you will be doing everyone a great service.

Websites and intranet sites can be anything from leisure destinations, to indexes, to dumping grounds for a lot of extraneous information. You need to make sure that your systems distribute information to the people who want it. This requires some intelligence, but is ultimately simpler.

summary

- networks distribute information to where it is most needed
- only communicate information to people who will find it useful

LOOK FOR THE WORD 'NETWORK' on the alt.quotations archives, one of many esoteric and usually useless sources of information on the internet and you will be given a quote from Guy Almes: 'There are three kinds of death in this world. There is heart death, there is brain death, and there is being off the network.'

For network in this case read the internet.

But in the world of e-business the word has another powerful meaning – it means the electronic infrastructure that underpins everything the company does, be it on the internet or a company intranet.

The network here equates more to Martin Luther King Jr.'s comment on society that: 'We are caught in an inescapable network of mutuality, tied in a single garment of destiny. Whatever affects one directly, affects all indirectly.'

In the network infrastructure of a company what affects one sector directly almost certainly affects most others, many of them directly rather than indirectly. And that network infrastructure is based on telecommunications and hardware that support the business and link each separate activity within it.

Since the days of Alexander Graham Bell commerce has relied on telecommunications to drive its growth on a regional, national and global basis, whether by telephone, telegraph, or wireless means. But not until the birth of the internet did telecommunications become the very epicentre of a business method: and telecommunications companies become the key to future global trading power.

The telecom wars that marked the end of the 20th century and the beginning of the 21st were about the internet and global domination; they were in effect the first world war of the new era. World War III.

Years ago some companies – Simmons & Simmons, the law firm we quoted earlier, is a prime example – recognized the coming war and developed a forte in the telecommunications field. It foresaw the convergence of telecommunications, IT and media concerns into global power blocs, and singled out the provision of communication business as one of the principal mainstays of its own international expansion.[1]

> “communications is about more than just which telephone company is used to convey messages from a to b”

Such corporations are repositories of accumulated wisdom in the network infrastructure field, and as such are prime sources of information for the e-company.

In this new world communications is about more than just which telephone company or telephony supplier is used to convey messages from A to B. It is about the whole communications infrastructure, including the hardware, the intranet, the extranet and the internet service provider which will link an enterprise to the international market it is trying to tap.

For one inescapable fact is that in a wired world (or even an unplugged one on the internet) all the computing power and data in the world are meaningless without a reliable and secure form of connection to the internet and to the areas of the company that will be involved with it.

From the very first dotted ‘i’ on a business plan, a company has to decide how much it is prepared to spend on hardware, what kind of website it wants to offer and how many visitors it anticipates. It has to think to the future: think to the possibility that what starts out as a little acorn in the suburbs of some small town will become a giant oak, spreading its shade over huge regions – and that the demands for its products or services could be unimaginably greater than anything it has hitherto dreamed of or longed for.

This is not as simple as it seems. The brief history of the internet is strewn with examples of major companies that failed to understand the awesome power of the medium they tried to harness, and came crashing down because of it. Even the mighty Encyclopaedia Britannica fell into the trap, as we noted earlier.

In 1999 when it decided to revive its flagging fortunes by putting its product online so that students, researchers, and everyone else could tap its articles free, it was so inundated with demand on the very first day that its systems simply gave up the ghost and crashed – and were out for more than 20 days. Encyclopaedia Britannica was selling nothing directly so its business was not irreparably harmed. Nothing more than its pride was hurt.

But eBay, the online auction giant, has estimated that the series of outages caused by massive demand for its services in 1999 cost it as much as $5 million, serious money in some companies' language. It does not even need to be as serious as an outage to cause damage to a company whose business is on the internet, simple frustration may be enough.

“at worst, there are outages, the cyber equivalent of 'Road closed for repairs'”

The amount of data that travel through internet network connections is measured in bits per second (bps). Regular domestic bandwidth measures about 30,000 bps, but a large corporate could use a bandwidth of up to 45 mbps. In other words, if domestic bandwidth is the size of an alleyway, then the corporate bandwidth is a 750-lane freeway – and even this, an exact mathematical ratio, may not be enough to take the strain of the traffic that could flow. If it cannot, then – at best – slowdowns happen, the equivalent of fender-to-fender traffic crawl. At worst, there are outages, the cyber equivalent of 'Road closed for repairs'.

The frustration of waiting for the traffic to move, or the road to be repaired, may be enough to make customers look for the nearest exit lane from the freeway. Road closure for a few days means they may never bother to go that way again.

In any start-up e-business it is the job of the head of IT to make certain this does not happen, and in the planning stage to cope for the unexpected, taking guidance from the input of the project manager along the way. Together, they should evaluate the network, check the internal and external infrastructure, ask how it will get in touch with its suppliers and cope with the rush it expects from its customers. And they must decide on how much the company is prepared to spend on its hardware, and what kind of site it wants for its money. For built into these considerations is the route they take in getting answers.

As the UK Institute of Directors said in 1999 there is nothing to stop a small businessman buying a computer, a modem and suitable software, designing his own web pages with a proprietary package and having that serve his company needs. For that the only additional help he needs is that of an internet service provider to provide the link between him and his customers and his suppliers to the web.

But on into the wider world there is a network to be considered: more than one man, or one department to be integrated, and the quiet life can vanish.

oh! what a tangled web

The bigger a company is before it starts its electronic exercise, the more it may stand in need of professional advice and training. Because the aim must be to link all communications systems, internal and external, so that they talk to each other, and to customers, paving the way for total integration of an entire business operation.

It is not as easy as it sounds. Ask Intel.

CASE STUDY

When Intel went into the reorganization of its global network in 1997 it knew that when complete the system had to be integrated in an overall, rather than a piecemeal, approach that would enhance its workflow and improve its customer relationships along the way. It needed to be in the productivity and efficiency game.[2]

One of the primary goals was to enhance Intel's competitive advantage by giving its customers better tools for managing transactions and data. At the same time, it expected web-based order handling to deliver tangible benefits closer to home, including rapid order fulfilment, lower overhead costs, and a streamlined process that increased operating efficiencies.

Another thing was clear: Intel needed to craft a solution that could work with a broad range of customers and provide a system of information exchange. Customers needed lots of technical information about the products, and inside Intel the various marketing and sales programmes needed business information to be sent out, but also to be made available internally.[3] And much of that information was highly confidential. Intel provides its customers with technical information it does not want to be made available to all and sundry: customers give Intel information about their future plans which they do not want to get into the hands of their competitors.

Prior to the web there had been a complex process involved in such information exchange – a staff-intensive process that needed to be eliminated, while the function remained.

In the minds of Intel executives back in 1997 a whole series of elements came together which, en masse, said that moving to the internet was better. Intel had to cope with one other reality: its customers never shut, and it could not afford to shut either.

First, it focussed on automating its order management system. For customers involved in the pilot deployment, web-based order management made doing business with Intel easier -a compelling and immediate benefit. It looked on it as adding value to the web commerce link.

It began delivering personalized information to its customers, including management, procurement, engineering, and marketing. The automated order handling and delivery had the extra benefit that both Intel and its customers were able to allocate major resources – in the shape of the people who had performed these duties – to less repetitive tasks.

The new e-business system also had to work within existing constraints. In particular, it had to conform to standard web technologies while remaining compatible with Intel's existing systems and enterprise resource planning (ERP) applications.

To avoid show-stopping disconnects, Intel began with a strict policy of standardization, to reduce costs while avoiding complexity. It bought its servers from a single vendor, specified a single operating system, and limited the number of database and development tools used in the project. At the same time, its group built in as much flexibility and forward-looking scalability as plans would allow. The ability to grow the e-business system was critical because it needed to be deployed throughout the organization. Simultaneously, issues of security and uptime were both paramount. A breakdown in the system would lead to intolerable disruptions in service.

To ensure always-on service, it installed site-level backups and established mirrored servers at alternate locations off-site. The pilot deployment went live with about 100 medium-sized original equipment manufacturers (OEMs) and distributors in some 30 countries. More than 65 per cent of the e-business accounts operated outside the USA, and Intel immediately reaped cost savings through reduced international phone and fax calls.

The customer response to the programme was equally immediate. Intel had set a 90-day deadline for transitioning revenue to the web, but that goal was met within just 15 days. It is, without doubt, a classic study in e-business deployment.

While many of the benefits of a web-based e-commerce system are obvious, the challenges in delivering such a service take planning and foresight. In Intel's case, key understanding of what was needed at the time, and for the future, drove its development, and largely helped it build up its network infrastructure requirements as it went. It designed its e-business system around what its customers said they wanted, meaning that even the pilot deployment focussed more on customers' needs than on Intel's own short-term goals. It was amazingly prescient for its time. It took advantage of the internet's ability to generate feedback, allowing the company to see what was getting used, receive advice and recommendations and complaints, and revise its plans and goals to suit.

In particular, it made sure it tested the performance and reliability of its customer web communications, across 30 countries, in a real production environment. This meant testing the communications lines, the circuits and the servers, the hardware and all the linking bits and pieces. It could not afford for one to be non-functional. One non-working segment would have made the whole collapse.

Intel's infrastructure had to carry a massive amount of sensitive material, all of it essential to the functioning of the visible network as a whole.

It could not post cookie-cutter content. Its customers were used to personalized, point-to-point service and the programme had to deliver accurate, current, and appropriate information for each one, often in bulky, resource-hungry quantities, even if that meant a multitude of different content arrangements.

It knew that security was paramount, but it recognized that a labour-intensive system for managing passwords and authorizations would be limiting. So it chose to adopt an automated process to manage passwords and entitlement to an encrypted system, which allowed it to verify the identity of each customer and authorize the customer to use the system.

All of this stretched both hardware and software to the limits available at the time and it placed massive demands on the expensive infrastructure in the communications world.

Intel was later to say that, in retrospect, the most valuable lesson learned from its e-business revolution was the need to balance costs and risks.[4]

Creating an intelligent system that handles human beings across a global reach, never sleeping, never tiring, and (hopefully) never failing is expensive, but it viewed the investment as critical if Intel were to continue to deliver lasting value to its customers.

The moral for all other companies taking the same route is that an e-business redeployment is not a short-term win: it is a long-haul, long-term business investment.

data centres, dark networks and flight paths

Many e-businesses organize their telecommunications, and infrastructure themselves. Like Intel they have the in-house knowledge and capability and prefer to develop systems in a way they believe keeps security under their own locks and keys.

Others go to companies that will do it for them, companies that will host their sites, and provide the network infrastructure in a relatively painless, if not inexpensive, way. There they will inevitably find that the world of network infrastructure is tied up with a whole lot of new IT buzzwords – resilience and reliability, total availability, mission critical.

The vexing problem is, that while they may be hard for the CEO of a traditional business, or the newcomer to the e-business world to understand, all of them are important.

“an e-business redeployment is not a short-term win: it is a long haul, long-term business investment”

One often forgotten aspect of e-business is that on the internet a company does not know where its customers are coming from, or even what time of day or night they are approaching it from. That means the system has to be open for business around the clock, to all geographic areas. If the system is down it is like having a ‘Closed’ sign on a shop door – the customer will look for a shop with an ‘Open’ sign hanging in the window. And once the customer has gone somewhere else on the internet to shop, he or she is unlikely to go back to the shop that was closed again.

This is where the data centres come in. Past the individual company hardware, past the unique server are the hand holders of the internet network infrastructure world, the hosting organizations.

Let's go back to Exodus.net and the airport.

Planes go in and out but while they are actually on the ground in the airport they are managed: they are guided to a slot, passengers boarding or leaving are processed by the airport staff and computer systems, and when the plane is full again it takes off.

Airports in the e-business world are effectively the data centres that apply in the virtual world: centres where everything coming in and out of a company is received, processed, and turned around again.

> “the data centre is the beating heart of the network, the flight path of the airline system”

The data centres of the giant hosting companies are physical entities: they exist in a real geographic space, and without them the virtual world would not operate nearly as efficiently on its global basis. They can be wondrous things.

Exodus, one of the world's biggest internet infrastructure companies (though far from the biggest), had 21 of them scattered around the world at the start of 2000. Within each one are hundreds of what are called cages, inside which are stored the servers of their customers – as many servers as the business needs to keep its operations running inside one, locked cage.

The centres are temperature controlled, earthquake proof, and bomb proof. They are patrolled by guards.[5]

Just as in an airport, ‘passengers’ or companies coming into the centre go to the equivalent of the check-in desk (the cage), locate their plane (the server), and fly to a destination through the system, land and go back out.

That is the physical structure of what in this virtual world of e-business is called a secure network – physical machines stored in physical, locked cages and the only people who have access to the cage are the customer and the technical staff who need to go there for servicing issues.

The data centre is the beating heart of the network, the flight path of the airline system.

But this is no fixed flight path. Just as with an airline there are alternatives to cope with the unexpected. Just as in the real world a network infrastructure company will have dual 'flight paths' across the Atlantic, so that if one is crowded with other 'planes' its traffic can take the second route.

(Such networks use dark fibres rather than proprietary telephone lines. They lease dedicated circuits – communications routes – from telecommunications companies which put the actual cables in the ground, or under the sea. Dark fibres are the plain fibres – when an operator leases the lines and puts optical networking equipment on it that 'lights' it up.)[6]

The dual-route system provides another entrée to the buzzword infrastructure – the mission critical and resilience bit.

how many elephants in a mini?

With dual paths across the Atlantic, or any other great stretch of physical geographic barrier, if there is any kind of problem, data organizations running systems for a company have an alternative route along which to send traffic. If a dredger cuts one of the undersea fibres, or a farmer ploughs up one on the land, then there is another route for the traffic.

The data centres are built to what the industry calls M+1 redundancy – meaning in simple terms that there is no single form of failure. If something goes down there is always something else to kick in as a backup or a bypass. These are the types of systems used by the giants such as Yahoo! and AoL.

The third element of network infrastructure is the management of the operation – in the airport analogy air traffic control, refuelling, and all the support systems such as electricity and catering.

It is the management of the system which balances the traffic, sorts out the planes in the air, diverting them to other airports if the original destination is blocked, and then leading them back to it over a different, unblocked route.

It is also the part that keeps a system flying when the traffic load gets intense – such as the time when *Playboy* ran a lingerie evening in November 1999 and 563,000 visitors logged onto its site to view it, at the same time. That traffic was handled and managed through an Exodus data centre.

“theories are the fault-line on which catastrophes are erected”

(Other web events, such as NetAid, have seen millions access the site at the same moment, posing enormous strains on the management techniques of the hosting company.)

Which raises the question of how many elephants can you get in a Mini? Or alternatively how much data can you actually shove down a line?

The answer is that, theoretically, in this kind of multiple handling system, the service is limited only by the amount of equipment available to service the databanks. Theoretically, there is no limit on the amount that fibre optic cables can carry, given that each fibre, the width of a human hair, can handle around 40,000 telephone calls at a time. But theories are the fault-line on which catastrophes are erected.

A data centre does not work on theories – it works on the more practical approach that, like the airline at the airport, there is a finite number of passengers who can fit into a particular model of plane. It also knows that at peak times it will get more than that number, so it puts on more planes to service the passenger load. Unlike the airline, it always has more available.

This is a world where sitting stranded at the airport, waiting for servicing, means lost orders and lost business. No company can afford it: no data infrastructure company can afford to be saddled with a reputation for allowing it.

But the wondrous part is that for a company that chooses the hosting route, all of this is invisible – both to its own staff and to its customers. It is the gentle facilitator, the central processing unit at the heart of a distribution system. It is the corps of engineers in a military campaign, keeping the roads open, the bridges up, and the fields clear of mines and craters.

No self-respecting general of a major electronic-based business should go to war without consideration of one.

nibbled to death by ducks

In a very different context Eric Sevareid used to say that dealing with network executives is like being nibbled to death by ducks. Anyone who has ventured into the business world of television knows exactly what he means: a little peck here, a little peck there, a long time dying.

> “dealing with network executives is like being nibbled to death by ducks”

A company that does not look to its networking infrastructure runs the grave risk of being pecked by thousands of indignant and irate customers, tired of outages and downtime or being unable to get through on a line whenever they want to.

It may be a long time dying. But die it will.

notes

1 See Chapter 3.

2 Interview with Ian Wilson, Intel, January 13, 2000.

3 As we said in Chapter 4, these ranged from those with small businesses to international corporations, from those who had never touched a computer to firms with huge IT departments.

4 Interview with Ian Wilson, Intel, January 13, 2000.

5 Interview with Phil Collerton, Exodus.Net, January 7, 2000. The earthquake proofing is even built into the data centres in the UK, not exactly prone to earth-shattering tremors. That is because the earthquake proofing is a design element, and it is more expensive to take it out than to make the data centres comply with the original standard.

6 In 1993 the city of Stockholm created a corporation called AB Stokab to build and operate fibre optic networks. In Stockholm today, as in Milan, there is a fibre optic network running through nearly every street. In Stockholm ISPs and new operators do not have to dig up streets to provide new networks, they just connect into the Stokab network. One of the results is that Stockholm is home to broadband services that provide unlimited high-speed internet access, making it one of the most e-business-conscious cities in the world.

a twilight home in australia: security

"Keep our troops covered as long as possible. Since we are always open to attack... we must at every instant be on the defensive and thus should place our forces as much under cover as possible"

Principles of War

General: Principles for Defense.[1]

FIFTH PRINCIPLE

security is a canard

'Security' is a scary word. Would you like some security? Of course, we would all like to have some of that.

It is only because people have not done the work required in principles 3 and 4 that security is an issue at all. We have all heard stories of businesses unwilling to put up a website because they are worried about security. It is like printing a brochure and then locking it in a vault rather than mailing it out.

We have all sat through the same presentation: 'they' might break in, 'they' might run off with all your customer information and sell it to your competitors, 'they' might sabotage all your data. First, who are 'they'? Disgruntled employees? Spotty teenage hackers? International spy rings? Or demons designed to part you from your money by building an emotional barrier to entry in the e-marketplace?

If you have done the work, then you know where your critical data is and how it is being communicated and used. Securing that data and those communications is simply a technology problem, as is creating business processes to ensure that security. It is only because we are unsure where our critical data is and how it is communicated that the security vendors can create the myth of the evil 'they' who are out to plunder your unsecure data. Yes, there are unscrupulous people, disingenuous people, people who might even pay to get to your data. You should assume that. But you don't have to build a Fort-Knox-scale security solution for all your systems. What do you keep in your safe deposit box at the bank? What do you keep in a strongbox at home? What do you leave on your dressing table, or on the seat of your car when you have dinner? Would your business really shut down if someone stole your customer list? All your former employees have one.

The internet is not an open gate or an unlocked door, it is a communications tool. You need to build security which is appropriate to the value of what you are protecting. And you need to remember not to let anyone in your organization turn security into an emotional hot button that slows down your progress in e-enabling your business. Solutions do exist, it's all just a matter of technology.

summary

- if you have followed principles 3 and 4, security does not have to be scary
- don't let anyone make you afraid that the evil 'they' are out to get you
- security should be appropriate to the value of the information it protects

ONE OF THE INESCAPABLE FACTS of the internet is that from its womb in the distant past it was designed for openness. Security has to be bolted onto it.

Which brings us to Barry Humphries, and the words of his alter ego Dame Edna Everage: 'My mother used to say there are no strangers, just friends you haven't met yet. She is now in a maximum security twilight home in Australia.'

When the internet was a meeting place for geeks and techies it is quite probable that there were no strangers, just friends waiting to be met. But when it stepped over from the techies' club into the world of business the issue of security was there staring it in the face, waiting to introduce it to the white-coated staff member in the Antipodean retirement establishment.

Few issues have been so exposed to the public gaze over the past few years as that of security on the internet. The media, online and off, have been full of tales of the exposure of the personal and financial details of customers, from their real identities through to their credit card numbers, sometimes through the inadequacies of the systems employed by e-merchants, big and small, sometimes because hackers or crackers have broken into sites to steal data, just to show they can do it, or with criminal use of those data in mind.

Time after time reports have suggested – and equally been denied – that the internet is a criminals' plaything, and that no one is safe from assault on his or her virtual person in these internet, e-commerce days, and no company is safe because its confidential data is just waiting for a hacker to strike.

At the visible end the hacking attacks, or data losses through negligence, may be real, or overblown, but the real damage in any company which has been found wanting in the security area is its credibility, its reputation, and its capacity to retain the trust of those who use it, a fundamental issue of business.

In days gone by our forefathers relied on wax seals and locked boxes to ensure confidentiality of a document in transit. Today's technology is their wax seals, and locked boxes, and just as keys to locks come in different shapes and sizes and degrees of effectiveness, and are used for valuables of different types, so security technology comes in shapes to match the degree of security required.

> “there is no such thing as total security”

At the lowest level there is the simple password – albeit that even in the best of worlds this is not so simple, as anyone who used the internet in the old days, when ‘usernames’ were a combination of letters and figures up to a dozen in number, will recall. This is little different to the encryption keys built into many software applications – making them impossible to open and use by anyone who does not have, and is not entitled to have, the key.

But beyond passwords come all manner of technologies, some with names that are all but incomprehensible to the average user, and certainly the average CEO of a potential e-business: public and private key infrastructure (PKI) and non-repudiation software, digital certification, and the rest.

What has to be borne in mind at all times is that there is no such thing as total security. Not in the real world, not in the cyber world, not in life. As Confucius said (and didn't he have a saying for everything?) the superior man never forgets that even though he is resting in safety, danger is not far away. [1]

Security is based on fear and emotion. Fear of what could happen, and an emotional response to the possibility, even though no breach of security has occurred. And that can cloud clarity.

Is security in the e-commerce world really more of a problem than it is in the off-line sector? Is a credit card more vulnerable going through cyberspace over an internet connection on a desktop personal computer than one taking the same route from the telephone in the restaurant, linked to the scanner on the counter?

Because we can see the scanner, watch the card being swiped, and then physically take back our credit card, does that inherently make it more secure than typing details into what is effectively the same technology in the home or the office?

And is the ability of a would-be thief to copy down numbers from the transaction slip in the restaurant, or at the call centre, any different to that of the handler at the cyber end?

From a consumer point of view it might even be argued that the cyber shopper is in less danger, given that the transaction is automatic from the keyboard to the company to the processing unit at the credit card issuing base, with no human intervention along the way.

“the ultimate security is an understanding of reality”

Be that as it may, it is not the public perception as countless surveys have attested: and the strong argument that an individual's perceived view of the insecurity of the internet is more magnified than the real insecurity of the internet is of little value to the electronic business if the consumer still stays away because of it.

Companies must weigh this public perception against the inescapable fact that nothing in the world is, as we said earlier, totally secure. The ultimate security is an understanding of reality. [2]

the other side of the razor wire In the electronic world people talk about firewalls and similar software systems as the great gods of defence in security issues. Build your wall in an electronic fashion, top it with the cyber equivalent of razor wire, broken glass and electrified strands and, so the theory goes, no one will get over to be savaged by the guard dogs standing as a second line of defence below.

But go back to basics. Treat the internet as – at its very basic element – an extension of the real world, another shop window. In the old days of doing business, before the buzzwords, what was the basis on which a company made transactions – even before the contract stage? Some say it was trust. Based on a person-to-person relationship. The old idea that a man's word is his bond. But always with the caveat that either side in a contract reserved the right to do background checking for their personal reassurance.

Take the case of a giant supermarket. When it wants a supply of mushrooms for its chain in a region it doesn't go to *Yellow Pages* and look up mushroom farmers, then call one and say, 'Supply me with 100 tonnes.' It carries out a vetting process. It goes out and checks the mushroom farm, makes sure the conditions and the product are the quality it needs them to be. Then the buyer shakes the mushroom farmer by the hand and says okay. A bond of trust has been created between the buyer who has seen the mushroom farmer and his produce, and the farmer who has seen the buyer and knows his company

Which brings us back to the cyber world, and the idea that business in the electronic age still carries the basics of its inheritance from the real world, that in the cyber world a man's word can still be his bond – even though the business, or the consumer, cannot see the face it is dealing with, or hear the voice at the other end of the phone.

The internet is an environment where a company rarely speaks with, or even sees, those with whom it is doing business, and the first thing anyone in an e-business or e-payments infrastructure needs to know is whether the person he is talking to is the person he believes him to be.

In the atomic world there are photographs and other kinds of ID. A legitimate customer does not go over the razor wire and the electrified fence, or brave the slavering guard dogs waiting for dinner beyond. He walks up to the front door, shows an ID and at the lowest level of security in most businesses that is enough to get him through to the person he is scheduled to see. But if he has no authority, if he is getting in for other reasons, there are fake IDs, there are ways of disabling the electrified fence, using supports to cover the razor wire, putting the dogs to sleep.

And what about the stuff coming out of the company? What safeguards the integrity of that? A suitcase chained to the wrist, or an armoured car in physical cases. But in the case of non-physical items, or for information, mostly companies relied only a couple of years ago on a shredder for paper and a fax machine for documents.

The cyber world has changed much of this. Nowadays the guards and the razor wire may still be there, along with the dogs, to guard against physical intrusion but most companies send their data over telephone lines, in the form of e-mails for the main part, relying on 'firewalls' that protect incoming data.

But in many cases anyone with computerized general knowledge, and having 'public exploring hacking' types of minds (that is, anyone between the ages of 12 and 18) can install an eavesdropping program on the other side of a firewall, the side that faces the public.[3] Which means any message that leaves a building through the firewall hits the eavesdropping program on the other side, is intercepted, and can then be sent anywhere in the world.

A company sending its quarterly results to key officers three days before they are to be presented to the market could have them intercepted, sent out, and acted upon, and then retracked without the company being aware it had happened until sudden trading in the shares indicates something is amiss.

Which is why one person interviewed for this overview on security in the e-business world said frankly that he held the view that e-mail today is less secure than writing confidential information on a postcard, throwing the postcard into the street – hoping that someone will pick it up and pop it into the letterbox – then having it delivered to the address without anyone changing what is written. The postcard, he suggested, is more secure than e-mail because if it is changed, the receiver knows it: with an e-mail he doesn't have a clue.

In the cyber world, encryption and firewalls are the equivalent of the atomic world's fence and dogs: they are first lines of defence but they only stretch some way down the chain. At some stage there has to be what the industry likes to call 'risk management control' which means old-fashioned secure ways of bolting on face-to-face (or in this case data-to-data) security options.

“at some stage there has to be what the industry likes to call 'risk management control'”

Those inside the business need to know, when they get an e-mail with an order, that the person sending it is authorized to do so, so that the company can get on with whatever it is necessary to do, whether it is process a payment, order supplies, or just pass something on down the line. In the old days that was where trust came in: the farmer had shaken hands with the buyer and both accepted that the other would fulfil his part of the bargain. But even in the cyber world the buyer's handshake with the mushroom farmer, the one that created the basic element of trust in the first place, can be replaced.

The handshake is the equivalent of what in the cyber world is called a 'digital certificate' – a token that each trusts the other. Under the digital certificate system everyone, in time, will almost certainly have a digital certificate of identification much as in most of the world people carry identity cards, or as in the USA a social security identification document. Even in Britain, which has stood out resolutely against the idea of ID cards for decades, the government now issues plastic

National Insurance cards with a personal identification number to everyone approaching the minimum working age of 16. It may say it is not an ID card and should not be used for identification purposes, but the number is unique and identifiable.

“exchange of digital identities across the internet will become a universal method of identification”

Exchange of such digital identities across the internet will become a universal method of identification. To some extent, and in several places, it already has.[4]

But even with the digital identity as common as the social security number, the identity card number or the electronic signature, there is still a need for management of the risk. An army, arguably, has within its ranks the greatest security of all: but even an army's security can be breached, and the wise commander posts patrols to secure his positions, even when he is in friendly territory.

a back street in singapore

In the real world, the supermarket buyer, after the handshake, has no real way of knowing whether the farmer will go round to a mate a couple of kilometres away who grows mushrooms in his old pigsty or to the garage that grows them as a part-time sideline, and use them to make up quotas.

But the buyer goes ahead with the deal because of the trust he has established. That's the real world.

In the cyber world, without risk management, the shop window could be the pigsty, or a garage in a back street of Singapore or elsewhere, and the e-mail seemingly posing an order or transmitting information of a sensitive kind could be coming from anyone, anywhere. And even with an electronic signature as a unique identifier, at this early stage of the game it is far from widespread, and equally far from foolproof.

For some companies the answer will lie in going to a company that specializes in security – or risk management as most call it – and delving into the world of digital certificates.

The use of a digital certificate is a bit like taking along a notary public every time a company executive goes to hand over some confidential documents. It is a way of giving an element of authority to the probability that the executive is who he says he is, and comes from the company he insists employs him.

Digital certificates work with the e-mail system most companies now use for business and data or document transmission and involve putting a simple verifying regimen in place. They use what are called public and private keys. In the brave new world they will come at birth, along with a social security or identification number, perhaps the one replacing the other. The public key, which everyone can know (some companies publish the public keys they issue online, like a telephone directory) is used to encrypt a document – and the private key, which only the holder knows, is used to decrypt it. The private key can be on a smart card, or installed on a receiving machine, so that it automatically decrypts the incoming messages that are tied to it.

> “security, like ice cream, comes in many flavours and, like liquor, in many strengths”

The end result of using the system is that if a message intended for someone in particular goes astray, anyone who receives it will be unable to decrypt it, and will see only gibberish.[5]

In a digital certification system the sender types out his e-mail in plain text, with extensions or add-ons or whatever else is required. Using the public key of the person to whom it is being sent the text then goes through a hashing algorithm that essentially cuts it down to a smaller size, turns it visibly into a mishmash of incomprehensible type, and assigns it an electronic signature.

Technically simple. Nevertheless, getting the message across to people that it is both simple and secure, that it helps create and maintain public confidence, is likely to be a long time coming. Companies that set themselves up in the public key infrastructure (PKI) business years ago now hardly try explaining what is happening when they sell the system to companies.[6] Instead they sell the idea of trust. Mushroom growers, supermarkets, and back streets in Singapore.

the PIN cushion

Security, like ice cream, comes in many flavours and, like liquor, in many strengths.

One of the buzzwords in the security world as the century tipped was 'strong authentication', a grandiose term for identification.

Every time a customer goes to a bank's hole in the wall to get cash, takes out an ATM card and inserts it into the slot and types in a personal identification number (PIN) technology then uses the information, and the card together to identify the customer.

If the two fit the money comes, if they do not an error message flashes up, and it is time to try again. A digital identification system everyone knows and most people are comfortable with.

Some of the most secure online verification technology works in exactly the same way: a customer uses a PIN and what is called a 'token', but unlike a digital certificate this token flashes a number that changes every 60 seconds. A user inputs the number into a handheld device, which is time synchronized with the server, and if the right number is keyed in in the right amount of time it will authenticate that the person sending the message is not only who he says he is, but that he is actually holding the 'token'.

One of the buzzwords in the security world as the century tipped was 'strong authentication', a grandiose term for identification.

CASE STUDY

When Boston's Beth Israel and Deaconess Hospitals merged, they realized that they needed a way to offer doctors quick, easy access to medical records from both hospitals. They came up with the notion of 'CareWeb' – an intranet providing a consolidated view of the individual systems of the merged hospitals. Before CareWeb, if doctors at one hospital needed information from the other hospital, they had to wait for the information to be faxed or read to them over the phone – a process that could take hours rather than a few seconds. It was not just a matter of general information and routine transfer – the easier access to patient records provided by CareWeb could not only save time, it could save patient lives.

'The problem with creating an intranet', said Dr John Halamka, executive director, CareGroup Center for Quality and Value, 'is that the public perceived that the internet was a very bad place to store medical records.'

The last thing the hospital administration wanted was to see in the local newspaper a headline reading '*CareWeb Reveals Sensitive Patient Records.*'

It needed a network guaranteed safe from break-ins but one that would not inhibit doctors' access to the vital patient information. Without an air-tight security solution, the project would never have got off the ground.

'We were charged with finding the best technologies – the best of breed – and putting them together to create a single, secure system', said Dr Halamka.

In its quest to get it right, the hospital turned to RSA Security Inc. and its secure ID token system. Under this system a doctor had to have a hardware device to access pages on the company's site containing patient data. The tokens were small, handheld credit card-sized devices with LCDs, containing microprocessors that calculated and displayed unpredictable codes. These codes changed at a specified interval, typically 60 seconds.

The process meant that every user had to start a session entering a user name, a memorized personal identification number (PIN) and the currently displayed pass code from the token. The algorithm that the token used to generate this pass code was synchronized with the RSA server that verified the pass code for each particular 60-second period.

Once through the user was authenticated for duration of the web session, or 15 minutes, whichever was less. This 'two-factor authentication', combining a PIN with a one-time pass code made it virtually impossible for a hacker to access the system. And if a token were lost or stolen, it could be immediately deactivated for the entire enterprise by disabling it at the server.

Because the password on the token changed every minute, it made the whole system much more secure than one which used the kind of static passwords that many people still share or write down near the computer terminal. Such practices defeat the authentication, access controls and audit trails offered by unique user names and passwords.

In the Beth Israel Hospital case the complex system had an unexpected security side benefit. Although newspaper articles highlight the threat of computer break-ins by unauthorized hackers from outside the organization, the truth is that data access from *inside* any organization is even more common. And in the hospital environment normal human curiosity leads those not involved in a patient's care to look up the records of VIPs, celebrities, and fellow employees receiving (or having received) treatment.

The Beth Israel system made sure that authenticated users could be held accountable for actions taken while using the system by setting up retrievable audit trails that log all accesses, to information, including time, date, information accessed, and user ID. And patients have the right to demand to see the audit trails. Bingo! Spies or just the curious can be tracked and held accountable for their actions.[7]

The PIN and token system also means that in an increasingly non-centralized work world, remote workers, signing into a central system, get authenticated. Authentication is a key to all kinds of remote access projects, and part and parcel of the aspects of security that must be addressed. And this security can apply to industries and to situations one might not immediately connect with internet possibilities.

The construction industry has been slow to move into the electronic world, with engineers preferring to stick to architectural drawings and blueprints in the old ways, rather than view them on-site on portable computers, even though the online system allows such drawings to be delivered from a central site direct to everyone who needs them, in any part of a site, without wasting time or money waiting for them to be commercially printed, packaged, and delivered. One of the problems always cited is security: companies not believing that their drawings, quantities, estimates or other products needed for the job will be safe online.

CASE STUDY

When the US construction company Webcor (founded in 1971, long before the web – so its name has nothing to do with the internet) started to build a $50 million, 12-storey office tower in Santa Clara, California, it found it needed to link the owners in New York, with the architects and engineers in San Francisco, and those on-site in Santa Clara. It used the e-commerce site, Cephren, to co-ordinate the site activity, which stretched not just across thousands of miles but different time zones. The entire construction team as well as owners and others involved were given encrypted passwords enabling them to enter only that portion of the Cephren site assigned to their particular project: there they built their own content.

The passwords allowed for differing levels of access to information and services – a middle manager could post a request for information but not see the minutes of the senior project management team's meetings, for example. Blueprints and drawings were all available in secure form, as well as communication through controlled e-mail.

Webcor President Alan Ball said that the estimated cost savings through the system were about $50,000, but would have exceeded $200,000 if all of the subcontractors and suppliers had been online. In two years, he said, the use of such secure sectors online, accessible through a site, would be mandatory.[8]

Webcor had an advantage. It is located in Silicon Valley and Ball had seen technology in operation for years, and trusted it. And in the end, underscoring all the technological means available to a company to enhance security, ultimately so much will still depend on trust. Not just in the technology but in the people involved in any business operation.

“at its basic level security is about the risk management of trust”

No one would buy a used car from a man at a garage on an old scrapyard site who keeps winking his left eye every time he says that it has a guarantee and was owned by a little old lady who kept it under cover except on the Fourth of July every year when she took it out for a spin to the end of the drive and back, and, look, the mileage is only 4.7 even though it's 20 years old. Everything in trading or communications, across content, community and commerce ultimately involves an element of trust. And at its basic level security is about the risk management of trust. Which is why one of our interviewee's advice to business was to move the old trust model onto the internet.

Don't change a thing; just let the technology do it for you.

shrink wrapped or tailor made? When it comes to security, as with anything else in the e-commerce world, there are always alternatives.

At the PKI level there are companies that will supply the shrink-wrapped version, and those that will offer the tailor- made, bespoke version. The shrink-wrapped version is self-explanatory: a box of tricks (or rather a box of software) handed over to an IT department, the company pays it money and then goes about setting up its operation itself.

The bespoke version will be more complex. This is, after all, a question at basic level of risk management. It is a question of retaining the trust that a company has built up with suppliers, and intends to build up with more, and which has taken time and effort and considerable money to acquire.

Bespoke companies will try to understand what a company is aiming to do, and just why it is trying to do it. It will try to find out what risks the company already runs and deems acceptable, and what risks it wants to cover, and those which it is prepared to continue to leave to chance.

Those are then integrated into the solution that is provided.

On the surface that could be simple: but companies may have different levels of security on the software they already use; they may have different servers and different software programming. They are not going to change all of this just to ease the take of a company they are paying to provide a secure platform: they expect the solutions company to know that different browsers, even different versions of the same family, need differing security solutions.

It will design and deliver a Lamborghini, not throw them an off-the-shelf Ford Fiesta.

Whatever package, whatever route, the elemental fact is that security is a factor which must be taken into account in the e-business process. These are the issues that everyone who heads an IT department must address when deciding on any system for e-business. But project managers, sales directors, marketing directors, and finance directors must equally accept that they have to have a part in the way it is approached as well.

The danger for some companies will be that paranoia over security among its executives, especially those steeped in the old ways, will stifle the whole project.

That is when it might be as well to remember the words of Helen Keller, who said: 'Life is either a daring adventure or nothing', adding, 'Security does not exist in Nature, nor do the children of men as a whole experience it. Avoiding the danger is no safer in the long run than exposure.'

Those who believe, like Michael Dell, that e-commerce is war may prefer the more succinct phrase of General Douglas MacArthur, who said:

> “There is no security on this Earth. There is only opportunity.”

notes

1 'The superior man, when resting in safety, does not forget that danger may come. When in a state of security he does not forget the possibility of ruin. When all is orderly he does not forget that disorder may come. That his person is not endangered, and his States and all their clans are preserved.' *Confucius: Laura Moncur's Motivational Quotes.*

2 H. Stanley Judd.

3 Interview with Simon Lofthouse and Bob Carter, JCP/Trust base, Sun MicroSystems, January 21, 2000.

4 On July 1, 2000, President Bill Clinton signed into law the Electronic Signatures in Global and National Commerce Act, which made digital signatures legal in the USA. In this case, no particular technology was specified for the identification procedure – Clinton used a card with his actual signature on it, scanned into a machine and embedded into a document, to demonstrate the possibilities. The other options available at the time included thumbprint scanning or third-party products using encrypted keys – essentially scrambled code – that can be attached to e-mail or electronic documents.

On July 10 a similar bill (and a similar gimmick) was signed in Ireland by President Mary McAleese. Fittingly, the Irish digital signature included software from the Irish leader in the field, Baltimore Technologies. She signed with a click on the signature and saw a 'thank you' message appear then commented: 'A polite way of doing business. It's the first time anyone has said thank you to me for signing a bill.'

Nevertheless according to Anthony Abboud, at the Chicago law firm of Wildman, Harrold, Allen & Dixon, it could be 2005 before the system is commonplace, given the need for many companies to install the infrastructure they may need.

The legislation enacted does not force companies to use electronic signatures. It left that to the marketplace, along with the problems of creating security around digital transactions.

But within days of the US signing iLumin Corp. in Utah claimed it had used the digital signatures in the first end-to-end home purchase.

5 Even today wrong numbers are part and parcel of using a telephone: in the cyber world mis-addressed e-mails are just as common. So many companies have names that are

similar – we were told of one person who at Christmas 1999 received the entire business plan, with all the business contacts and a strategy for the next six months of a British company. Because it was not encrypted it could be read by anyone who received it. It had the same name as a totally unconnected company in the USA – the only difference being that the American company had the letters USA at the end of its name. Whoever sent it had forgotten to add those three letters.

6 There is a longtime closed public key infrastructure system which the public and business have been using for years without recognizing what lies behind it – the systems of Visa and MasterCard. They are called closed systems because they are independently closed to each other; one card cannot be used through the other's systems and both are so big that independent banks take their systems, rather than create their own. That was changing in 2000 with the advent of Identrus, formed by a number of worldwide financial institutions to facilitate the growth of business-to-business electronic commerce.

The institutional partners were ABN AMRO, Bank of America, Barclays Bank, CIBC, Chase Manhattan, Citigroup, Commerzbank, Deutsche Bank, Dresdner Bank, HSBC, Industrial Bank of Japan, NatWest, Sanwa Bank, Scotia Bank, and Wells Fargo.

Identrus claimed to be the first organization to establish the necessary components, both technological and operational, to enable companies worldwide to address the trust and risk barriers impeding the wider adoption of e-commerce in sophisticated global business transactions. It leveraged the unique positions of its members as the traditional agents for commercial collaboration to add a legal and business framework to traditional PKI.

Identrus provided for legally enforceable e-commerce transactions within a framework where all the participants could manage risk, establish a uniform global system of rules and operating procedures binding both sides of any transaction (signing and relying) and provide a well-defined dispute resolution process and recourse mechanism.

The oversight comes in because the financial institutions are regulated, and local government and police authorities preserve their existing jurisdiction to enforce agreements between contracting parties. Financial institutions like banks see themselves as the ideal providers of identification and identity risk management in the virtual world. They have the experience, the infrastructure and the resources needed to facilitate global business-to-business e-commerce. They also have the tradition of bridging the 'trust gap' between trading partners.

The question, in the latter half of 2000, was just how the credit card giants would react to this intrusion of a minnow on the global internet payment table. Would either of them buy the fledgling operation, and any others that sprang up in its wake? Or would they adjust to the virtual world themselves?

7 Interview with Mike Awford, RSA Security. January 21, 2000.

8 Bob Tedeschi, *Chicago Tribune*, July 11, 2000.

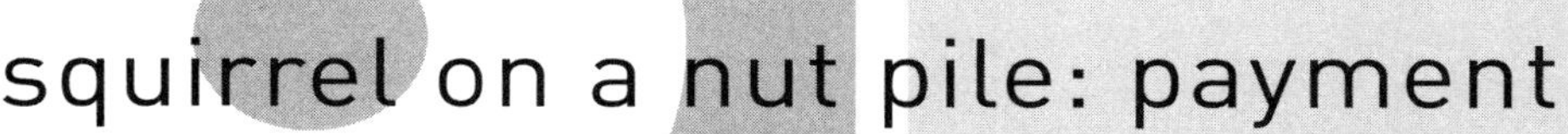

8 squirrel on a nut pile: payment

> "Not all positions are of equal importance: the most important are those in which we most likely may be attacked. It is here that we should have all the advantages, while in others we may need only part"
>
> **Principles of War**
> Principles for the Use of Terrain 15

he who pays the piper...

Accepting money over the internet today is as easy as swiping a Visa card. You can negotiate with many vendors to absorb as little or as much of the security and fraud risks as you like – it is just reflected in the transaction costs.

Visa, MasterCard and many of the other bankcard companies are happy to take your business. Your bank, the vendor of your accounting software, the e-marketplace you just joined, all will line up to arrange payment for you.

SIXTH PRINCIPLE

Let them. If you are going to take money online then someone has to clear the transaction. All you have to do is to fight for the best deal, which is purely a matter of negotiation. These companies will offer intangible benefits in exchange for a percentage of your revenue. It is still early in the online revenue wars, and they want your business. Watch out though, because many of the offers out there are like the sucker bets in the middle of the crap table – designed solely to bump up the house rake. Their favourite way of doing this is to use security issues that appeal emotionally, but often turn out to cost more than they are worth.

But the standards are falling into place. Most accounting packages will allow electronic fund transfers and clearing – even on a daily basis.

summary

- the bankcard companies will queue up for your business
- negotiate hard and don't allow them to play on your fears

ALAN SCUTT IS THE FIRST TO ADMIT he is no Martin Luther King, Jnr. But he, too, has a dream.

He dreams of a day when consumers accept, without thinking about it, that they can take anything they see, anything they want in the physical world, and buy it online.

This is the day when the internet will have become part of everyday life, when people will be going to the personal computer or the television that has interactive internet built in or through the old set top box, to book a table at the local restaurant, order a holiday, use a service, and take it as second nature that all they have to do is click with the mouse.[1]

You find the site you want, select the product you want in the size and colour, make the payment and then within days the product gets delivered and your credit card is debited, and you have a good experience and go back to do it all again.

And his second dream, naturally enough, is that when it happens they will do it all through his secure payments company.[2]

In any business enterprise the handling of the little matter of payment is at the centre of any transaction. It is the squirrel on the nut pile.

Forty years or so ago, a shopper walked into a retail store, had a look around, chose a shirt from the rack, or pointed to it in a box on the shelves behind the assistant, then handed over cash to pay for it at the till. The salesman pressed the keys, the drawer opened, and the money handed over was lodged and change given. The assistant wrapped the shirt, inside its box, in brown paper and put it, perhaps, into a bag, and the satisfied customer left with it under his arm. And at the end of each day someone had to add up all the money in the till, take away the float, and that was how the salesman knew he or she had sold £200 worth or whatever that day.

It was mechanical. And the only way the store could tell it had actually sold a shirt instead of a pair of knitted long johns was by doing monthly, quarterly and six-monthly stock checks.

In time that moved on: the assistant, the mechanical till, and the parcel wrapping vanished: the customer paid for the shirt with a credit card that was swiped and no money changed hands. Only the stock checks remained and they were no concern of the customer.

> “in any business enterprise payment is at the centre of any transaction. It is the squirrel on the nut pile”

In today's cyber world the software handles real-time credit card processing, builds in robust internet fraud protection, and generates online reports. It has back-end integration, storefront integration, shipping/tax calculation, and caters for delivery of digital merchandise.

It enables the customer to pay for the item. It processes the charge, even makes a direct deduction from the bank in the case of a debit card, then goes on to perform all the back office functions such as restocking, unseen by anyone.

It does this in a way that is simple, transparent and seamless – the first hurdles in overcoming consumer reluctance to shop online. In the off-line version a customer just picks up his shirt and his card and goes elsewhere. In the online world the process goes a little further, with the customer sent verification e-mail and a note perhaps telling him a delivery date.

The strange thing is, given how payment is the very life blood of any transaction, and paying is as common as eating, few companies selling payment software systems have found a way to articulate online payment in a way that is palatable to client companies mired in traditional outlooks. The best do not try: they offer the e-business instead a system that they can demonstrate, which it is obvious customers will find easy to use, and which the company will find reliable and that will bring them as few headaches, and public relations setbacks as possible.

In the case of an e-tailer that is purely online it also has to work on a global basis – a consideration that the assistant in the old traditional store rarely had to take into consideration. If the sale was for an item which involved overseas transmission, under the old system it was simply handed on to the overseas department for all the necessary, complicated, legal and financial work to be done. Today the software should be able to handle that as well, at least in part.

Payment solutions work in a simple enough manner (even though a little jargon is necessary). Once a customer hits the 'buy' button, or the assistant in the off-line shop hits the till button that is its equivalent, the merchant establishes a connection to the payment solutions company's engine using secure sockets layer (SSL) protocol as the security barrier.

Depending on the specific requirements of the merchant's business, the program modules for tax and shipping and fraud protection are brought into play, other functions are performed and then the payment part (module) of the software makes contact with the credit card processor and credit card authorization is completed in real time. If it happens to be an overseas order the software can also build in the various customs requirements and paperwork. The state of the transaction is simultaneously logged in the database for recovery: in a pure online operation, such as when a consumer is buying from the site of a bricks and mortar retailer, the customer is notified via e-mail once the sale is complete and when the goods are shipped. After credit card settlement the transaction is stored in the database and fulfilment systems can be updated.

The customer sees nothing. But the software tells the company that its invisible, unpaid online salesman has just sold a shirt, size 15, blue stripes at £50, the customer has paid by credit card, and the transaction verified. It does not have to be sent to Abu Dhabi, but it will be waiting for Federal Express to deliver next day or the day after.

At any time of day the back office knows how much has been sold by menswear that day, and how many shirts have been sold.[3]

But in the new world of e-commerce it goes even further: the shirt is still sold, the credit card swiped, and the detail captured: but the sale is linked to the accounting system, to the inventory system: the inventory is automatically updated, new supplies automatically ordered.

The beauty is that under ideal conditions it takes between three and seven seconds and the consumer does not have to worry about a thing except clicking a button, and typing in some personal details. It is no more arduous than signing a credit card slip in a restaurant or physical store. But for the e-business it provides a system that keeps operating costs low, and profitability high, with 24 hours, 7 days-a-week availability, data integrity, fault tolerance, and scalability. It also offers a way to minimize loss from fraudulent orders, which result in bank chargebacks and processing fees for the merchant.

It is how payment issues work in the internet age.

the red light means stop Bricks and mortar businesses do not charge fresh faced into the e-tail world.

> “bricks and mortar businesses do not charge fresh faced into the e-tail world”

They have developed good business systems over the years, support an infrastructure that is established, with inventory, invoicing and accounts and for most of them e-commerce is an extension to that operation, not a replacement. Most neither want, nor always need, a complete new infrastructure in the cyber world. What they do need is the ability to integrate all the operations so that there is no interruption in the flow from the customer to the order, to the payment, to the delivery, right through to the replacement of the stock.

They need a payment system which integrates behind the scenes with all the existing systems, whether they come from the same company or not. And that comes replete with the normal security problems that exist even in the real world, where credit card fraud, and counterfeit notes are still merchant issues.

In the aforementioned old days when the bricks and mortar stores were built, customers came in with cash, paid for what they wanted, and if it was paper money it was held up to the light to try to check if it was genuine, or counterfeit. Today a customer expects to go to a virtual store and type in a few numbers and find the product on the doorstep two days later (if not within the hour).

“there are still fraudsters who will use credit card numbers illegally, and in the online world that presents different problems”

That makes it easy to buy, which is what the merchant wants, but what he also needs is integration with his existing systems (the equivalent of the cash drawer, the trip to the bank, and entry into the ledger) and protection against fraud. There is no banknote to hold up to the light, but there are still fraudsters who will use credit card numbers illegally, and in the online world that presents different problems.

In a high street store if a consumer goes in and carries out a fraudulent transaction with a credit card, stolen or forged, the merchant is protected. In an online transaction when a consumer uses a stolen number, he is not: if the transaction is a fraudulent one then the credit card company counts it as a ‘card not present’ transaction – and refuses to refund the cost of the purchased merchandise.

Worse, when a bank detects such a fraudulent transaction it will charge the merchant at a higher rate than it normally does for processing his cards – and if there are numerous fraudulent charges against him the bank will blacklist him as well.

This is why merchants need top-level payments systems that offer protection against fraud by intensive checking.

But through today's payment solutions providers functions have been added that the old style retailer had to install by instinct: they can add in their own rules.

In rules-based payment engines a merchant can decide if he does not want to sell to people with certain physical addresses or postcodes. He can refuse to sell to a certain IP address, or even an e-mail address or at a certain time of day (although there is always the little matter of discrimination to worry about, as Wells Fargo found in mid-2000). But this is not a blunt instrument: it does not mean blanket exclusion, which could result in many lost sales. It is a sophisticated arrangement under which the merchant establishes rules which can, if he wishes, permit progress through the chain under additional conditions.

And it has no real equivalent in the atomic world.

Such software works like a set of traffic lights: if it detects certain things happening – a blatant fraud for example, or use of a credit card number that has been reported stolen, or if the attempted purchase is from a customer, or an area that the merchant has, for whatever reason, blacklisted – it can put up a red light for stop.

Sale halted.

Or if it is just a little concerned – say at a product ordered at 3 am from a distant location – it could give it amber, and divert it to a call centre so that a physical operator can intervene and check out the delivery. That enables a company to safeguard the possibility of a sale just by further qualifying it with human intervention. It also means that with an expensive product which is beyond the limit of a customer's credit card, a call centre operator can quietly suggest another way of paying for it.

Sale safeguarded.

Then if everything is fine it can give the green light and pass it on for processing and delivery.

Sale made.[4]

It does not stop there. Such fraud protection modules are already leading even further down the e-business trail. They are also becoming marketing devices, driving steadily towards inbuilt ability to help a merchant identify safe selling and buying patterns, giving him the chance to target potential safe customers, and keep away from those who, in the past, have popped up as dubious in the fraud modules.

And like many other functions in an e-business plan, tapping a secure payment firm for provision of such services means also tapping into their accumulated wisdom, with the possibility of unforeseen value-added benefits.

In 1998 Britain's Eddie Jordan, of the Formula One Grand Prix racing team, did not have a website. He did not think he needed one. He couldn't see the need for it. His business, after all, was motor racing. But it was suggested to him that out in the wide world were millions of Team Jordan fans who wanted to learn and understand about the team, and they needed somewhere to log on and find out about races, drivers, and the cars. He accepted that and when the site went up he started to get millions of hits on Grand Prix weekends when fans wanted more information about what was happening.

One weekend Alan Scutt went along to a Grand Prix race and the first thing that struck him was the way fans were buying up Jordan merchandise – hats, sweatshirts and so on. It was a short step from there to persuading Jordan that if only half of the millions who visited his site on Grand Prix weekends were actually to buy something, it would be a major business return. Jordan went for it: he installed a merchant payment engine, branded the Jordan name across the internet and now has a major new source of income.

The advice came free with the engine.

don't worry about the hype Without payment there is no business: without secure payment any business there is is fraught with dangers.

But secure payment is an area beset with acronyms such as EDI (electronic data interchange), SET (secure electronic transaction) and buzzwords such as e-wallets and micro-payments, all incomprehensible to many CEOs and all elements of the hype that has come with the 'e-commerce' term.

The message that most should remember is that way back in the 1980s, some people – such as Warner Blow, President of Sterling Commerce in Dallas – started to use the words 'electronic commerce' to differentiate from the kind of electronic trading that many companies were already doing under the name of electronic data interchange (EDI).

“without payment there is no business: without secure payment any business there is is fraught with dangers”

And since then not a lot has really changed in fundamental payments trading terms, except the way the funds are transmitted. In 1999 Sterling Commerce, concerned at the way that the hype was worrying traditional sectors, even began to take out ads in major magazines telling the business world that they should not worry. But what has changed is the consumer perspective.

Today the term e-commerce drums up in the mind of the general public the thought of selling books and CDs online, of trading securities over the internet, of buying and selling at online auctions: to veterans it is just another way of looking at the electronic data exchange that they were handling 15 years ago on an international banking and corporate level.[5]

Where things have moved on for them is the communications method – driven by the worldwide telephone connectivity and by wireless technology and the way that mission-critical business is now linked through interweaving technology and applications. Where once it was done directly, business to business, it is now done over the internet, making security paramount. And the message they now preach is that technology has a real value when married to a company with business experience and expertise. Technology married to a company with no business experience or expertise is a losing proposition. (Unless they bring in some from outside.)

> “what has changed is the consumer perspective”

If a company is building mission-critical systems, integrating its internal systems and its customers and suppliers, what really counts is the knowledge of how to do that, not the technology. After all, the technology changes. It could be a different technology altogether in five years' time.

Knowing the communications software, the actual EDI networks, the translation software, and the tools to integrate business with the processes, that is what matters. Which boils down to the advice that there are many things the hype is overlooking but that people who are running business have to take into account.[6]

In the end, the key for business is the way that a secure system removes people from the process, sitting them outside the day-to-day functioning.

look ma, no hands!

Most of this chapter has addressed the question of secure payments from the point of view of a business selling to a consumer: but the principles are the same whether it is business to consumer (e-tailing) or business to business. Somewhere in the chain payments have to be made.[7]

The future is about business applications talking to other business applications, computers talking to computers. It is about computerized applications exchanging data in an automated fashion every day, day in and day out, without human intervention, and releasing expensive staff so they are free to deal with services to customers that add value, such as analyzing customer buying habits and how they can be better served.

People should be moving.

> “a company wading in e-commerce waters and wanting to succeed has no choice but to investigate widely”

A company wading in e-commerce waters and wanting to succeed has no choice but to investigate widely and find the type of process best suited to its operation that allows it to receive payments securely from its customers and to remit payments equally to its direct or indirect suppliers.

The process will obviously vary depending on whether the company is in a business-to-business environment with monthly accounts or in a business-to-consumer market where payment is needed before delivery. And it may vary to reflect the size of the transaction undertaken. These are all issues for reflection by, and to come under the control of, the company finance director and head of IT. But sales and marketing directors need to be involved to ensure that consideration is optimal for their customers, and the purchasing director needs to ensure that consideration is optimal for company suppliers.

When it comes to facing the music, however, the buck still stops with the finance director and head of IT.

This is not the end of the payment principle: many other factors come into play, from the issues of how to handle small payments that are too insignifcant for the credit card to handle (the $1 and $2 pops) to those of how to set up systems which can still attract payments from those who have no credit card – not just those who, for whatever reason, do not meet a credit card issuing company's criteria (which can be as insignificant as having no credit history because everything has always been bought with cash, through to relocation from an overseas address), to those who are too young to hold them.

The internet has solutions to these problems, in the shape of micro-wallets, and parent-controlled credit top-up facilities, the equivalent of cyber allowance, and to every other payment query a merchant may have.

We concentrated in this chapter on security because it remains the biggest issue in the minds of the public, and of the businessmen who want to trade on the internet but cannot quite trust it.

Von Clausewitz said that war is part of man's social existence, more accurately compared to commerce than to art or science, because 'commerce is also a conflict of human activities and interests'.[8]

In this conflict of human activities and interests one thing is constant. Ultimately someone pays. The e-merchant needs to make sure it is not him.

notes

1 In the UK Alba introduced television with internet access built in June 2000.

2 Interview with Alan Scutt, Clear Commerce, January 6, 2000. Clear Commerce is an Austin, Texas-based provider of E-commerce transaction software for nearly 15,000 merchants, including Apple Computer, E-Stamp, Cooking.com and Chase Merchant Services. Its software features real-time credit card processing and robust internet fraud protection, as well as online reports, back-end integration, storefront integration, shipping/tax calculation and delivery of digital merchandise. It can support thousands of merchants on a single server, and process concurrent transactions at peak performance even during high-volume periods.

3 All of this is now part of the off-line world as well, where a retail store is integrated with the internet and all the processes take place in real time.

4 Interview with David Bruce, Northern European director of Sterling Commerce, January 6, 2000. Sterling Commerce is a Dallas, Texas-based company that now has 2,500 employees in 37 offices globally. It provides solutions to problems of making the transition to an internet-driven economy, including how to build and manage global commerce communities, how to better integrate their business processes, and how to achieve greater competitiveness through new sales channels, improved productivity and enhanced responsiveness to customers.

5 Ditto.

6 Ditto.

7 Despite all the headlines about fraud, most people in the western hemisphere pay online by credit card. But in the process of the interviews for this book some interesting points emerged from the experts in the payment field. They told us, for example, that as late as 1996, some UK banks were telling would-be entrepreneurs and e-commerce merchants that it was both politically and technologically impossible to take credit card payments over the internet (interview with Gavin Breeze, Datacash, January 19, 2000). By mid-2000 the UK e-commerce sector was not only built on credit card payment systems by consumers, but was ahead of the USA in that it was delving faster into smartcard technology making purchasing over the net, through a slot-in smartcard, inherently safer and swifter. Such cards carry a microchip embedded in them with details of the user's identity, credit ratings and limits, and have the ability to deduct from bank accounts directly. But the same sources said that UK bank managers at a local level still know little about e-commerce, and as of the start of the 21st century staff at two of the major UK high street banking organizations reportedly did not even have the ability to send e-mails from the workplace. Most of the development of e-commerce payment systems has been in the hands of small independent companies.

8 On War, Carl von Clausewitz, page 149.

9 scales of unhappiness: buying

> "The provisioning of troops is a necessary condition of warfare and thus has great influence on the operations, especially since it permits only a limited concentration of troops, and since it helps to determine the theater of war through the choice of a line of operation"
>
> **Principles of War** Strategy 13

SEVENTH PRINCIPLE

the first link in the 'value chain'

The migration of buying to the web is getting a lot of media attention, with the purchasing hubs and the multi-billion dollar valuation of companies such as Arriba and Commerce One.

Rather than thinking about the transactions, think about the relationships. Your company has invested resources in developing relationships with all the companies that supply you with the goods and services that you need to make your goods and services, whether they are widgets or ideas.

You need to know how those relationships were built, and which of them are critical. You should also wonder whether you can build processes that make the transactions between your companies simpler and more efficient. Some parts of the relationship can be automated, some cannot.

The internet is often presented as a means of automating relationships, and allowing us to conduct the automated part of those relationships with no effort. Invisible connections guide the marketplace's invisible hand and make the pricing of goods more efficient. This view of the internet is especially to be seen in financial projections which assume that everyone else's margins will be eroded, but the efficient new technology will improve our own margins.

Hmmm... Well, unless you happen to be at the very end of a value chain, that rosy view isn't necessarily the case. Neither should you assume that there is no value in those relationships you are automating. You may be presenting .competitors with an opportunity to examine the relationships your company has and their value to your company.

Cisco relies on incentives that bring real benefits – such as cash – to the people with whom they have relationships. Once again, the technology is a solvable problem. What will ultimately distinguish you from your competition, is your ability to keep your strategies aligned with your maps. If you ignore the value of relationships, and enter into marketplaces where everything is a commodity and relationships have no value, then you make your company another link in a web of chains, and you must expect your margins to be pulled as tight as everyone else's.

And when the big order that has to be out by Thursday comes along, will your nameless, low-margin partners be there to make sure you can deliver? No.

Transaction costs have a purpose.

summary

- you have invested in relationships for a reason, don't throw them away uselessly
- look at which of your relationships is valuable; only automate those which don't add any value to your business
- remember that transaction costs have a purpose

ONCE UPON A TIME there was 'electronic procurement'. It was a system where an employee sat at a desktop, clicked on a button that said purchases or something similar, searched through a catalogue, built a requisition and got that approved inside the organization, according to the spending limit allocated to each executive level. Maybe it had to go through five or six layers of management approval, within the figurative four walls of the operation, but eventually it either got rejected or reached a clearance level. It had nothing to do with checking stock availability with a supplier, transmission of the purchase order, understanding the latest pricing or product information. Those were all aspects of a process that needed interactivity between a buyer and a supplier.

Neither did it link the buying process with the supplying process in real time: by its very nature e-procurement focussed on the buying organizations.

> “in e-business it is the balance between buying and supply that counts”

In e-business it is the balance between buying and supply that counts.

Today there is still electronic procurement, but it is an enhanced version that bears little resemblance to its ancestor.

In today's e-business world the technology allows the selfsame employee to sit at his desktop and search the catalogue through key words, drilling into it if it has technical specifications. The same software then creates requisitions, which in turn support whatever the approval process may be, with pre-structured approval processes where they are mandated.

But the employee can also check instantly to see if the item is in stock – no more picking up the phone to the purchasing department. Then, if he needs to write a confirmatory letter and fax it out, the software is available for instant use – no need to drop out of the system. He can go back and look at the status of the requisition, where it is in the approval process for example, and if it has been approved and sent out, he can check out the status of the order. No more hassling the purchase department to fax the supplier and give him hell. The software even builds in processes for receipting and payment.

What all of this new way of electronic buying provides is a way to empower the employee and through him or her the company: total electronic connectivity at a business level, allowing contact with the supplier in real time in different ways, without having to fall back on faxes, phones, even e-mail or more cumbersome methods.

It gives the company a way to automate everything, to make sure there are no hiccups in the system.

But only if it works.

In the old days, not so very long ago, the employee at his desktop would click on the button that said 'purchases' and the system would be down. He would report the matter and sit back, maybe, if he was conscientious, making use of the telephone and fax machine and scraps of paper to get around the problem while it was being fixed.

In today's cyber world that kind of delay cannot be tolerated: the system not only has to be infinitely better, and dramatically more comprehensive, it has to be far more robust.

Congressman James Paul, a member of the House of Representatives' Science, Space and Technology Committee's subcommittee on Investigations and Oversight was once involved in checking out the procurement system for the US Federal Government – at that stage non-automated.

Nevertheless he said that it was 'like a software system with bugs':

Every time it's broken down somebody has patched it. But keeping it together is getting harder and harder and costing more money. At that point an experienced software engineer would throw up his hands and say 'Hey! Let's toss this out and start over!'

In the e-business world starting over is the path to a raft of new possibilities – and for those who have to make the choices, a host of new considerations

let the software make the choices

CASE STUDY

Joe Public knows Kodak as a photo company: photographic enthusiasts also know it as a photographic paper and chemicals company. In reality it is an arm of Eastman Chemical, the global producer of fibres, plastics, and chemicals with over 16,000 employees worldwide. When it decided it needed to automate its annual purchases of more than $3 billion, Eddie Page, its Purchasing Manager, was the man on the spot. His decision would directly impact Eastman Chemical's bottom line.

Eastman saw three challenges.

First, the company needed to set up a web-based electronic procurement application, but simultaneously maintain operations with and between its existing ERP systems provided by German leader in the field, SAP. Second, it had to make outbound ordering among approved suppliers easier, and third, it wanted a cost-effective method to manage supplier catalogue content.

It needed to provide customers with the ability to search for supplies, select best-value items from contracted suppliers and easily create and submit a requisition. But it also wanted a system that was 'intelligent' – one that could make decisions, decide whether the request should go out as a purchase order, or if a requisition needed to be created and handled manually by purchasing staff, or indeed whether it could remain outside the legacy SAP system and eliminate the need for invoicing and other back-end activities.

In other words it had to be a system that would grow with the company and not become obsolete in a year.

That meant providing automated flexibility to make choices on process handling, configured with criteria for purchasing, based on internal company rules and policy (such as putting a cap on dollar amounts for hands-free purchasing).

It had to assess multiple conditions intelligently, including whether the user had a credit card or if the purchase was under $2,000. Only with such information could the system determine the best method for sending out an e-commerce purchase order, keeping it out of the legacy operations, and eliminating unnecessary steps.

Eastman tried out Page's choice at its Kingsport, Tennessee, corporate headquarters with one commodity vendor (for office supplies) and 50 users. That number quickly rose to 2,509 and the company added a second vendor, for laboratory supplies, and began implementing it across major US sites.[1]

Meanwhile it leveraged the extranet portion of the solution that automates external supplier interaction through a real-time trading market to increase its supplier base. Until all of this it had relied on an ERP system, which sent out either faxes or EDI transmissions to suppliers, to handle its procurement processes, even though traditional EDI does not integrate well with the systems of every vendor.

Through its new technology, Eastman Chemical now maintains the advantage of real-time transactions without carrying the burden of multiple customizations and integration. Suppliers do not need any particular software, just connection to the web.

Because the system stores data on purchase and supplier behaviour patterns, it proves a strategic tool for negotiating favourable vendor contracts. And its purchasing card and electronic catalogue encourage employees to use only corporate-approved suppliers.

As a result, it has substantially decreased the volume of rogue purchasing and orders are getting back to the preferred suppliers at the contracted prices. Because order volume is increasing with contracted suppliers and that volume is then leveraged for increased discounts, overall costs are decreasing. It is the old circle.

Eastman Chemical is able to receive rapid responses, shorten fulfilment cycles and implement just-in-time MRO procurement strategies. The company can also improve inventory practices through its enhanced ability to gauge inventory levels that meet the real-world requirements of its departments.

It has, it says, directly improved the company's order fulfilment cycle and guaranteed best bottom-line savings. It helped Eastman streamline workflow and business processes for better order processing and tracking, bringing a tighter focus on supplier strategy and standardization of product selections.

Ultimately, it helped the company on what should be every company's goal – it optimized overall efficiency.

By June 2000 it had transformed the roles of their product salesman. Kathy Wachala, a principal account supervisor, then told the New York Times that she did not sell chemicals anymore, she sold the whole range of Eastman services:

'I identify Eastman's capabilities with those of our customers. Then I look for partnering opportunities – a manufacturing process we could help simplify, a new product we could help improve.'

These days she no longer heads a sales team, but a 'consultative team' culled from various departments released by the transformation to internet operation, with the goal of nurturing relationships to make customers 'more loyal, more profitable and more reliant on us.'

it's only ten pence dearer at rymans

In a business-to-business world the buying company should be looking for three main areas of benefit from an electronic business system.

First, it should reduce the cost of goods and services, by improving the compliance of the purchasing transactions with any strategic transactions the company may have made. Compliance is a difficult thing. Most companies have rules about who can buy what and where and when, and for how much – but making staff observe them in every little detail is easier said than done.

> “the buying company should be looking for three main areas of benefit from an electronic business system”

It is a no-brainer that by committing to volume buying a company can negotiate a cheaper deal than by shopping at the local retail store for an individual item. But it only gets any benefit if it actually buys from the supplier – in other words, if it puts out volume against the contract.

In a big organization employees know the proper process, but many of them very often cannot be bothered to follow it. They take the attitude, 'We have got to get on with it and we'll nip round to Rymans and get the slides we need because they are only ten pence dearer. Can't do any harm. Put it on expenses.' But when one scales up all those ten pence pieces over its entire operation – that non-compliance with purchasing process – it tots up to a lot of money.

The electronic way allows constraint on which employees can buy, who they can buy from, and what items they can buy. It can – or should – be quicker and easier for the employee to use the system, so encouraging as well as forcing him or her to use it and, as a result, reduce the cost of goods and services.

The second advantage lies in the ability to cut the overall cost of administering the process. Most purchasing processes for indirect goods and services are paper based and people based. They involve filling out forms, sending different copies to different people, leaving a paper trail around an organization. Employees and executives all the way up the ladder have to read the forms, sign them off, and ask questions about them. It is a laborious, time and talent-wasting exercise, which companies cling to because it is the way things have always been done.

In the electronic world this is automated, and the amount of money saved in time and paper forms can be huge.

In a traditional operation administration can cost around £56 an order. So, regardless of the value of the purchase, a £6 piece of kit could cost £62 because it would cost £56 to process the purchase. That can be cut to £3 or £4 through an automated process.

(Infobank tells the tale of a customer whose average spend on processing a purchase order was £55 sterling before they started using its integrated technology – and they trimmed it to £10 sterling in just four weeks.)

The third benefit is cycle time – the time between when an employee decides he needs something, and when the product or service actually arrives and he can carry on, by implication, being productive. In some industries a conservative cycle time between order and delivery is seven days: in an automated system it can drop to two, although it is difficult to compress that further given distance delivery.

“at its basic level electronic procurement is and always has been about making companies and employees more effective”

The knock-on benefit is lower inventory costs because a company no longer needs to carry such large stocks.

From the point of view of an employee it takes away the mundane bits of the purchasing jobs. Some people believe it will drive a shift in the role of purchasing, with purchasing value in the future more to do with strategic sourcing activities – finding the right suppliers, the most competitive suppliers, and managing them.

For some employees it will also mean being out of a job.

And for new ones coming it will need more computer literacy to be able to manage strategic buying: even more education in the elements and theory of business.

At its basic level electronic procurement is and always has been about making companies and employees more effective.

> “modern electronic procurement can do it faster, does do it better”

Studies done by the Warwick Business School show that 80 per cent of a specialist's time is spent on administration. Four days out of five that worker is doing paperwork rather than his or her job. The paperwork has, indeed, become the job. In today's electronic world that can be reduced dramatically. The result is cost cutting and that means money that drops right to the bottom line.

Stop for a moment and think what any organization would have to do to deliver an 80 per cent increase through sales revenues.

The message – modern electronic procurement can do it faster, does do it better.

never mind the buzzwords

The world of e-business is full of acronyms. In the financial services area they have SETs and EDIs, in the buying area they have ERPs and CRMs, SCMs and MROs.

But acronyms are nothing more than shorthand buzzwords for systems, or products, that are often indecipherable in their longhand form except to the professional involved in the particular sector, which in the atomic world of business purchasing means the finance, purchasing and operations directors.

Only a couple of years ago the word was ERP – enterprise resource planning (which was earlier called MRP (management resource planning). Then it was MRO – maintenance, repair and operation. Next came SCM – supply chain management, and in 2000 the buzzword was CRM – customer relationship management, or how to be happy and love your customer.

It is a kind of evolution of confusing buzz in-words.

But the truth of the matter is that, by and large, few people understand why or where customer relationship management fits in with e-business, and where supply chains fit with CRM. Or even what a supply chain is. (A group of organizations that buy from each other to complete an order that is sold to an end user, be it a consumer or a corporation. From the end user even back as far as the raw material. That's a supply chain.)

But what acronyms, and all the systems they encompass, have to address at some stage is the wider truth that whatever is done with a business it has to be driven by what a customer wants. No matter what the name, all customer-facing processes – and the ability to understand and manage them – come down to being able to deliver what the customer demands.

> “a business has to be driven by what a customer wants”

E-business is about matching the capability of a company, its products and whatever else it provides, to the needs of the customer and the potential customer in an interactive way. Or as one person once said, it is electronic matchmaking at its most basic form.

In the 1970s Swedish mathematician Martin Leindorfer took what today his executives at Industrie-Mathematique call 'pull driven logistics' and from that developed software for supply chain management. Nowadays it is called the 'Sell, Source, Ship' model – or if one prefers it the 'Amazon model', or the 'Dell model'. The older version was 'Buy and Hold', or so-called push marketing.

Selling, sourcing, and shipping is the new, pull-driven sector, and the internet is the ultimate pull-driven business model. Dell, with its direct marketing and lean inventory, where everything is sold before it is built, is the new; Compaq, with its need for inventory to restock retailers and requirement to manufacture then ship to retail outlets unsold, is the old.

Both have supply chains that furnish their raw materials.

In the most efficient systems, in order for any kind of supply chain to work, the direct suppliers of the company must be linked to the company's website before customers begin to buy the company's products. Without this any company runs the risk of supplier shortage and inefficiency.

And that means the supply chain has to be managed electronically also.

it's not the tools, stupid

Supply chain management has been called many things, mostly procurement, inventory, and logistics.

But that is a little like saying that marketing is about brochures and advertising. While these are elements of the marketing process, marketing itself is really about a conceptual way of doing business, about addressing the needs of customers in a profitable way. It is not about the tools, it is about the means of achieving the end.

And supply chain management is about recognizing that business is dependent on the network of relations that a company has formed, being put in place to address the needs of an end consumer.

The relationship between a customer and his supplier is elementary: a customer goes to a supplier who either meets his needs, or doesn't – and if he doesn't then the customer goes elsewhere. Theoretically, managing the relationship at this level is simple. The customer either gets the goods he wants on time, at the right price, in the right place, or he shops with another supplier.

From the supplier perspective, the relationship is more complex: he not only has to know what the customer requirements are in terms of product, but the price the customer is prepared to pay, the method he wants to use to pay, and the volume he intends to purchase.

But, perhaps just as importantly, a supplier needs traditional customer information.

He needs to know customer behavioural data: customer preferences, old-fashioned retailing information, the kind the corner grocer used to amass instinctively without knowing he was doing it.

If the customer is unhappy with something – whether it is to do with the service he is getting or something else – the supplier company needs to know – in the blunt but expressive words of Ceri Jones of Industrie Mathematique – 'What has pissed him off.'[2]

He needs a history of how he has dealt with this unhappy customer in the past, so that he is aware in advance of the pitfalls. Some people will be put off by inaccurate invoices, some by inaccurate deliveries – all these things make people unhappy, and there are scales of unhappiness where some things score higher with some people than others.[3]

When the company moves into the 'sell, source, ship' environment of e-business it needs the information even more desperately: it is dependent on its suppliers, and, in turn, they are dependent on the company for information about its requirements.

> “at the end of the modern e-business day, supply chains are about speed and profitability”

The speed of getting that information is far greater than in the buy and hold world, where there is time for errors to be righted, and where the lack of one component does not matter quite as much because there are 100 versions on the warehouse shelves.

If a 'sell, source, ship' company is talking to a manufacturer and saying it wants one widget delivered tomorrow it is not saying, 'Make 10,000 of the things and I will stick them into inventory' – it is saying it has a customer who wants a widget shaped like this, and 'I only want one or two of them and I really do want them tomorrow, otherwise I can't satisfy my customer.'

The dependency on suppliers is in real time, not the send-it-next-week-if-you-can-manage-it of the traditional world.

This is where CRM and supply chain management fit hand in glove to become two elements of the same thing – moving product through the supply chain.

At the end of the modern e-business day, supply chains are about speed and profitability.

Nothing more. But certainly nothing less.

the dummy with the inventory

The bottom line in all of this is that in the new e-business world companies need to operate a business model that is driving inventory towards zero. After all, where is the commercial payoff, what is the bottom line, in inventory?

> "performance information is how well a company is doing in satisfying customer requirements"

That brings in another buzzword, performance information – which boils down to the process of trading inventory for information. Customers provide information on what they want and how they want it, and suppliers provide information on how it can be supplied yesterday. Performance information is how well a company is doing in satisfying customer requirements, and how well suppliers are satisfying the company.[4]

Inventory is about buffer zones. It comes about because of inadequacies in a supply chain system – allowing for lead time here, lead time there, distances and anything else that can be used as an inefficiency excuse.

No one said, 'What a good idea – let's hold lots of stock so it can gather dust and go out of date and cost lots of money to finance.' It just came about because of the inefficiency of the supply chain. And suddenly business is moving to a situation where it is buying one, making one, selling one – then selling one, making one, buying one. All the inventory gone.

In time this will lead to the death of retail 'sales' which have become such a tradition in retail marketing because no longer will anyone have out-of-date, surplus inventory to sell off at a lower price.

No company should want to be the one left holding the 10,000 486 Intel CPUs because nowadays we are into Athlons and Pentium 4s and almost multi-gigaherz speeds. It does not even want to be the one that made a good deal on Pentium 2s because no one wants them anymore either, and soon no one will want the Pentium 3s that it may be itching to buy as well.

In the e-business world information provides the speed, and the system should provide the ability to be able to react quickly to any change in consumer and customer demand or fashion.

And no company wants to be the dummy with the inventory.

the zero sum game

In this brave new world what happens to ERP, the great god of business in the late 1990s?

Some will say it is a system so out of date that it needs the last rites read over it. But the fact remains that in the first years of the new century ERP is still very good at what it does – focussing on internal problems, and internal inefficiencies and eliminating them. It can still deliver benefit to the bottom line by eliminating cost, and inefficiency.

But it is purely internal.

It has done a great deal to provide a single database system, a single transaction-processing backbone which is good at managing the things it was put into place to manage – manufacturing, finance, and human resources.

But its market share is static and possibly declining in a world where business is being forced to focus on the external, such as how to retain customer loyalty, and improve market share, particularly in the industries which rely on fast moving commodity goods, consumer package goods.

ERP is weak on its ability to address the processes, things like supply chain management and keeping customers happy. It is weak on the ability to help a company go out and grab new market share, rather than help it handle the market share it already has.

In areas such as hi-fi, or consumer durables – items expected to deliver standard service for five or six years – the market mostly grows hand in hand with expanding population. And even though the population is doubling every 50 years it is still a slow way of expanding. In the UK in the year 2000 almost every home had a freezer or a washing machine: the market for such consumer durables was tight, and getting tighter given that manufacturing processes are improving so the ones already out there will not wear out quite so quickly.

This is what some observers and analysts call the Zero Sum Game – the stage at which a CEO looks at the situation, and is forced to recognize that his obvious market is not getting any bigger. It is growing at maybe 1 or 2 per cent a year because of demographic change and the stark truth is that if he wants a bigger piece of the pie he has to go out and take it from someone else.

They say there is no bottom-line percentage in the Zero Sum Game and the only way of truly increasing market share in today's fast moving world is by taking it from someone else – and if an industry is not focussed outwards it will lose out.

(For me, the Zero Sum Game is not credible. I argue that the internet itself creates expanding markets – as Amazon.com has already proved: it locates transnational markets, expands the overseas reach, even gets more people to read more often by making literature easier to order and cheaper to buy. While Amazon.com has very successfully grabbed market share from the old traditionalists, and become the biggest bookseller in the world, it is still creating new markets that did not exist before.)

What is clear is that no company knows what is going to happen in the future. The paradox is that this future which it does not know is the very one it has to plan for.

the road to hell

The e-business not only has to plan for the unknown and the unpredictable; it has to plan for it on a global scale, across multiple currencies and multiple languages.

This is where the internet is the key: the internet can enhance and exploit opportunities in the procurement sector when it is used wisely, and within the context of an automated and complete approach.

Otherwise, as Ceri Jones is wont to say, 'The web could well end up providing companies with just a quicker road to hell.'

CASE STUDY

Late in 1999 Britain's largest and leading supplier of commercial office products, Guilbert UK, with annual revenue of £300 million, moved over to an integrated e-solutions programme. The company has 150,000 corporate customers across seven European countries and a turnover of EUR 980 million. In the UK, it services the needs of 87 out of The Times top 100 organizations.

The language and currency demands it would make on any supplier of technology were critical to Guilbert, and in the end it turned for advice to a local UK company Infobank, whose technology supports electronic trade in multiple languages from multiple locations in multiple currencies from within a single system.

The technology automatically represents information in the language and currency of the buyer, at the same time as representing product orders in the language and currency of the supplier. For Guilbert it is a solution made in heaven and made it an apostle for the modern-day electronic procurement systems industry. It recognized that, beyond the dust storm, today's electronic procurement is not about the internet. It is still just about business.

It is about planning every aspect of every business process for agility and speed: for quick movement. It is about setting up a supply chain, and organizing its relationships and its infrastructure in a way that is consumer centric.

notes

1 Commerce One's BuySite, Desktop Commerce Application.

2 Interview with Ceri Jones and Eric Sidnell, Industrie-Mathematique, December 7, 1999. Industrie-Mathematique has been around since 1967, when it began operations in Scandinavia. It was born out of a logistics consultancy, and began to grow in terms of enterprise software in the 1980s. It entered the packaged software solutions arena in the late 1980s focussing on pull-driven solutions that were in demand in Scandinavia at the time. Its founder, Martin Leindorfer, was talking about pull-driven technology as long ago as the 1970s. It is now a premier European logistics services and consultancy company.

3 Ditto.

4 Ditto.

10 a little spend: supplier portals

"In spite of the new methods of provisioning it is quite impossible to do without any depots whatsoever. Therefore, even when the resources of the region are quite sufficient, a wise military leader does not fail to establish depots in his rear for unexpected emergencies and in order to be able to concentrate his forces at certain points"

Principles of War
Strategy: General Principles 16

now it's your turn

In the previous chapter we talked about the value of your company's buying relationships. Now it is your turn to consider your supplier portals : you must make sure your company is as good a partner as it can be to all the people with whom it does business. This is pure community building. You need to find new ways of integrating with your customers, so that every aspect of their transactions is as easy as possible.

EIGHTH PRINCIPLE

You need to consider whether your customers might want to make design recommendations about your products and, if so, ensure that it is easy. You need to go through the ordering process, making that as simple as possible. You have to make sure customers know your delivery timescales, and that these are reasonable. And to be really helpful, you should integrate with their financial software.

All this means looking at relationships as opportunities for co-operation – anticipating your customers' needs in order to fulfil them.

You should use technology to make relationships simple, by automating everything you can. You have to beware of forgetting the human touch – you should use the time you save by automating parts of the relationship to personalize the non-automated parts. Margins will flow towards the company with the best relationship base.

summary

- be easy to do business with

VON CLAUSEWITZ was frequently long winded. Napoleon said it shorter and perhaps better: 'An army marches on its stomach.'

And business marches on its supplies.

But an electronically engaged business marches on the cheapest supplies it can get, delivered from the widest spectrum of suppliers, all linking together to provide the most efficient and cost-effective supply option.

In leafy Bedford Square in London, David Graham, now Managing Director of BuyingTeam.com – otherwise Buy.co.uk – sat back one day in 1998 after weeks of reading about the inevitability of e-commerce and began to look at his company.

It was a consultancy, called The Cost Reduction Partnership, based in the atomic world and a niche in providing information on pricing – where to go for the cheapest electricity, the cheapest stationery, how to save money on bank charges.

“an electronically engaged business marches on the cheapest supplies it can get”

'It was clear to me that in several years we were potentially going to be under threat as e-commerce was fully implemented', Graham was to recall.

'Why would anyone need us anymore, if they could go on the internet, find out where the best pricing was, and how to save money – goodbye

Cost Reduction Partnership. I said, if that's going to happen I am going to be the one destroying my business.'

So he set up and registered Buy.co.uk and he moved over from TCRP to establish it.

What effectively had happened was that the advent of the internet had provided the tools and mechanism for the company to establish an online replacement for itself, to target small and medium-sized companies with technology to let its clients co-ordinate and aggregate their purchasing.

TCRP was, and is, Britain's leading purchasing consultancy. Its clients include the supermarket chain Asda, the high street retail operation House of Fraser, MTV, Sotheby's and other household names in the UK or abroad. Its raison d'être is to save companies money: big companies, small companies. On everything from office supplies and utilities through to cars, computing, staff, telecommunications, and travel.

Like most other companies in 1998 it looked on all purchasing as a glorified catalogue system, just as other major international companies still do.

But it is not.

Buying is a lot more. Reducing procurement costs is a lot more. It may be catalogues in terms of what a concern buys every day of the week, again and again – but with the internet it is a much more interactive system, and a more elaborate system but one which can still result in indiscriminate methods of targeting potential buyers unless it is co-ordinated.

Buying in the modern connected world is equally about having in place the systems, the warnings, the alerts that do not come indiscriminately out of the ether to advise of a last-minute holiday to a potential customer who only gets three weeks vacation a year, and they all went last Christmas.

It is about being alerted two months ahead of time that the international domain name registered two years ago is about to expire and unless you rush you may lose it – as JP Morgan, the international banking firm, did in June 2000 – but if you rush you may also be able to negotiate a better rate.[1]

It is about using the internet to make certain you do not miss something that is cost effective to your business.

> “buying is about having the relevant information filtered to make it usable”

Buying is also about having the relevant information filtered to make it usable: it is all very well having an alert from your technology about cheaper supplies for all that stationery you need – but if those cheaper suppliers are all in New Zealand and your company is on the Isle of Skye, what is the relevance?

Filtering moves the operation away from the general to the specific.

In the case of the stationery alert the purchasing consultancy will keep lists of clients relevant to a geographic area: it may have them listed all over the world but unless told otherwise it will only send its clients alerts about cheaper suppliers from two or three stationery suppliers, not the global list, and each supplier will be local to the client company region.

This may be a contradiction of the ethos of the internet, which deals in global outlooks, but is based on current marketing realities.

In 1998 a major UK charity approached The Cost Reduction Partnership and asked it to review the purchasing systems it was using. The charity ran several hundred sites across the UK. All of them were predominately autonomous in their buying, there was no professional buyer, and each site was, in effect, its own buyer for almost everything.

Each site had discretion in its day-to-day operations, and this philosophy had crossed over into the buying area. No central purchasing function existed. There was no control over the items bought, the supplier used or the prices they paid. There was no economy of scale in the buying function. Supplier reviews were infrequent and inadequate. On the rare occasions preferred suppliers were in place, not all sites were using them.

As TCRP dug deeper it found that thousands of paper invoices were being created at a local level, some were sent to head office, others sent to sites for authorization, then returned to the head office for payment. Suppliers who wanted to talk about any possible regrading of their accounts had no point of contact to discuss possible changes.

TCRT amalgamated the charity's buying requirements across nine basic buying areas, then reviewed and renegotiated preferred suppliers' contracts. Where there were no preferred suppliers, it put the consolidated requirements out to known third-party companies. All sites were told and 'educated' about the new arrangements; reasons were given for the changes along with the potential cost savings they would achieve. Controls were implemented to ensure that preferred suppliers would always be used.

It then set up consolidated billing of areas such as utilities through head office – an efficient system which had the added benefit of eliminating the risk of electricity or telephones being cut off to the various sites, as had happened in the old days of lost invoices and poor communications.

> “some organizations do not have the aggressive push to drive their prices down by white-knuckle bargaining”

It later estimated that the changes saved £330,000 a year for the charity on a national basis, and unspecified but large savings through administration and paperwork reductions. By the start of 2000 all sites had personal computers with access to the internet installed and links to BuyingTeam.com.

So in this world of reorganization, of upheaval, and of changes to the whole process of buying, where does the benefit lie for any company that goes into it? What can the buying company do that the client cannot do itself?

Theoretically, possibly nothing.

But Graham does not see it that way. Some companies don't have the know-how, some organizations do not have the aggressive push to drive their prices down by white-knuckle bargaining.

So how does Buy.co.uk describe its function as far as its clients are concerned?

Said Graham, grinning: 'We batter the shit out of suppliers on their behalf.[2]

how to save money and make a billion Supplier portals come in many shapes, sizes, and models. They call themselves supplier portals, buying portals, online exchanges, marketplaces, and vortals. But they all effectively provide the same service. They are customer-facing destinations for buyers to reach a full range of products.

In the dying days of the last century the industry got a new buzzword – the online exchange, or marketplace: within weeks it appeared as if every industry in the dictionary was racing to announce the coming together of large multinational corporations, to form platforms that would link to suppliers over the internet with the expressed aim of making massive savings in overall costs.

In early 2000 Forrester Research was predicting that there would be 10,000 such buying/supplying communities by 2003, and by the end of 2000 that already looked an underestimate.

Among the biggest announced in the first few months of the new century were those of the giant automakers (two rival camps, one led by Ford and GM and the other by Volkswagen), the airlines and chemical, steel and global retailing industries. The theory behind all of them is simple – to offer a single site from which a company can buy ancillaries that provide the 'raw materials' the employees need to produce a product or a service. A supplier portal will aggregate everything into one electronic catalogue, where goods can be ordered on one form, paid for and delivery expedited. The cost saving is fairly obvious: there is no need for multiple telephone links, multiple forms to be completed, or multiple warehouses where inventory is to be held.

Among the ancillaries, a supplier portal will allow for near real-time price comparisons and support multi-currency transactions. So it makes suppliers more internationally efficient, allowing them to offer better prices and better service to their suppliers and buyers: it is a no-brainer that it will facilitate cross-buying and selling if they are all connected through a community/organization-centric hub where each has immediate access to every necessary function.

Trading in point-to-point relationships, using the fax, or phone or personal contact, is simply an inefficient business model in the electronic age.

“trading in point-to-point relationships is simply an inefficient business model in the electronic age”

But not all supplier portals have to be on the grand scale: at the lowest level most are still catalogue based aggregations of what is available. This has, however, brought problems. Companies trying to establish their own supplier portals found that they could get catalogues for the same products from a dozen or more suppliers but each of them would use different formats. One would use 'blk' and another 'black'; in one format 'blk' would mean 'block' and in another 'black'. Pulling all of these different approaches together into one useable format from ten to a dozen suppliers is a people-intensive operation that is basically grinding donkeywork. And when the dozen suppliers become 2,000 suppliers, as with the multinationals, it brings nightmares.

Enter the companies that do the donkeywork.

Commerce One – one of the world's leading marketplace builders – tackles the problem by telling suppliers to submit their catalogues in a specific hierarchy, with nomenclature that it defines, and it then scales the system, and manages the catalogues.

> "enter the companies that do the donkeywork"

Its attitude is that if there is no scalable solution for catalogue management the whole project stops, because beyond a certain number of suppliers the task becomes too difficult for any company to manage.

The catalogue management companies have this as their core competency and are very good at it: and because they are, they can scale the electronic operations more effectively than any standalone e-procurement project.

But then enters the ogre of delivery third-party services to the operation – another aspect of automating the operation.

In a trading community there are not only buyers and sellers, there are shippers, such as UPS and TNT, there are those who provide payment services, trade credit services, taxation services, travel operations. This is exactly the same as in the real world – a trading community is not just a bunch of suppliers and a bunch of buyers attached to a portal, there are all the third-party services without which, in effect, trade could not really happen.

And if you are a third-party supplier, how do you market that electronic service? Do you go out and form individual relationships with each of the buyers and suppliers – an obvious nightmare – or do you make the service available to the portal where all the transactions are flowing and have visibility to all the buyers and suppliers at the same time?

Clearly this is the effective model. And for the new third-party services emerging in the e-commerce world, such as identity warranties and guarantees, it is the street on which to play.

Business-to-business issues are about how a company facilitates the whole trading process, a far cry from the business-to-consumer-oriented issues of how do you find people to sell to.

But even online, different trading models work for different categories of trade. When it is a question of high volume, the global online exchange comes into its own, linking tens of thousands of suppliers with the multinational; corporations which need their products to survive.

The marketplaces are essentially gigantic reverse auctions in which sellers post lower and lower prices on their goods on the website, to secure a contract. General Motors, Ford and Daimler/Chrysler made the splash by jumping into these waters first with a plan to combine their individual exchanges into a single enterprise to handle as much as possible of their $250 billion a year in purchasing.

On the surface a sound business idea making use of the global reach of technology and the efficiencies of scale and cost that can be achieved by eliminating repetitive ordering, clerical jobs and saving duplication in the paperwork. But the idea of a supplier portal/online exchange does not sit well with everyone.

When the Big Three automakers announced their plans, the reaction – after the dust had settled – was that they were only trying to cut their suppliers' margins.

Alice Miles, President of Ford's internet exchange operations, was quick to market with an answer and a press conference, at which she said that the cost cuts they envisaged would not come from savings on payments to suppliers, but from that inherent in putting 35 per cent of the procurement online, such as the mountain of paperwork and accompanying employee time.

Rather than affect the suppliers' margins the companies would work with their suppliers to find areas of duplicated costs. 'Instead of thinking of it as a weapon that is going to be used against them, we want everybody to think of it as an opportunity,' she said.[3]

But then, as a famous British court witness once said, 'She would, wouldn't she?'

life in the neutral zone

Between January 1, 2000 and the end of June about 600 business-to-business exchanges were started, according to the calculation of the e-commerce research firm Net Market Makers.[4]

Some, such as the one involving Ford and GM, or that with the airlines, united rivals who until a year or so ago would have seemed like the most unlikely of bedfellows. From Sears Roebuck to its French competitor Carrefour, from Hilton to Radisson and Hyatt, from United to Continental Airlines, all came out with announcements of pending global marketplaces, with old enemies now collaborating to cut costs out of their supply chain.

They came together in a perceived 'neutral zone' where they could shop and save costs without prejudicing their internal security.

Ford said at the time it believed it would save 5 to 10 per cent a month on purchasing costs as it adapted to online tools in the business workplace. (Visa claimed it had cut the administrative costs of buying computer hardware by an average of $100 an order – or up to 90 per cent – by online procurement methods.)

The *Chicago Times* had a particular interest in focussing on the then new phenomenon of online exchanges in which the process cuts out intermediaries, the middlemen who traditionally stand between buyers and sellers, because its hometown was built on middlemen.[5]

Its central location in the USA made it a natural distribution hub for national and international companies. Its futures exchange was packed with middlemen bringing together buyers and sellers. And some of its most powerful businessmen made their fortunes as middlemen, such as the liquor distributor William Wirtz.

But the online exchanges cut out the middlemen: they try to make them redundant – a force 7 shock on the Richter scale shook the heart of the city at the epicentre of the US Midwest economy.

As David Bovett, co-author of the book, *Value Nets: Breaking the Supply Chain to Hidden Profits*, said, it was a 'sea change for the industrial economy that is critical to the Midwest'.

The truth is that many middlemen add no value: the internet exposed this inefficiency (and bottleneck) and determined they were redundant.

In the Chicago area several did not wait for the aftershock – they began to create their own online exchanges, hoping they could make up for their tardiness in the expertise and offering services they had to hope customers would pay for.

Chemcentral, a traditional company that traded chemicals, coatings and resins to the chemical industry, estimated that unless it made an internet move it would lose 15 to 40 per cent of its traditional value. So it built its own distribution channel, Efodia (taken from the Greek word for 'supply'), to service 70,000 customers in 30 countries.

It then began to offer industrial supplies and services, from pumps and hoses to janitorial and office suppliers, attempting to become a fully fledged supplier portal to a variety of industries.[6]

“the truth is that many middlemen add no value”

DSC Logistics, which began life in the 1930s as Dry Storage Corp., saw the light in 1994, much earlier than many others. It began to reposition itself from being little more than a glorified warehouse storing goods for other companies into a logistics operation, where the bricks and mortar warehouses became a fulfilment link behind such companies as Swapit.com, an internet market for used CDs, DVDs and games.

It had its eye on neutral e-marketplaces that would need its add-on services for warehousing, transportation and tracking services, the third-party sector of such trading communities.

Ann Drake, the daughter of the man who founded the Des Plaines firm, but who, as its new CEO, had turned it around into being the largest third-party logistics company in the USA, said that 'all links in the supply chain are fretting about the implications of the internet.[7] The anxiety level is high. There are no pathways. We are all learning and making it up as we go along.'

buy me, I'm available Buying and supplying is not just a function of the world of tangible goods: it applies to the world of services as well.

In 1999, according to Forrester Research, the buying and selling of business services online amounted to a relatively insignificant $22 billion. But it felt that inside a year that figure would rise to $44 billion, and although still insignificant alongside total business-to-business transactions, it indicated a substantially growing sector.

Most of the services, it suggested, would be sold one to one by companies with established relationships and very few through the fledgling online marketplaces. The reason is that buying a service requires 'a chemistry between buyer and seller'.[8]

It also needs a deep sense of trust, when the services cover such complex and fraught areas as the law, or such individual and intensive services as creative design, where personal contact would appear to be an essential part of the process.

Nevertheless, this is a competitive world, and if shopping around produces a better, or as good a service at a lower price, then trading in human services, like trading in cows or sheep, means that the development of service marketplaces is inevitable.

Bruce Tonkin, an analyst at Forrester Research, has said that over the next three to four years he expects such services to take hold, because, 'Even the most complex, human intensive services will have an internet component'.[9] In his crystal ball, marketplace sales of human talent will rise tenfold over the next ten years, helped by the lack of emergence of an industry leader or model, leaving the field wide open.

Some idea of the potential comes from the experience of Free Markets, a company better known for its auctions on both sides of the Atlantic, geared to the business-to-business marketplace for tangible goods.

In 1999 it made $2.7 billion in sales through its site, of which $123.8 million was in human services, ranging from temporary workers, through to skilled installers in the telecommunications industry.

Mondus is an e-marketplace that operates in the USA, Britain, Germany and France, again mostly in the traditional sector. At the turn of the century it started to offer a marketplace for couriers and translators, and was breaking into the world of human resources, legal services and public relations.

From Minneapolis I-Radar set up its e-marketplace in late January 2000, connecting those who needed human services with the skilled individuals who could deliver them.

The supply of human services through an online exchange has inbuilt restrictions, however. If someone wants a lawyer he wants him from the local region – particularly so in a world that may be converging in many respects but still retains differing laws state to state, country to country. A company that needs a plumber is more likely to prefer one from the locality, so, too, an electrician.

But for a growing world army of designers, writers, and ideas suppliers the online marketplace is an opportunity to expand on a global basis. And the technique is simple – the people with talent, or services, to sell prepare profiles of themselves that are lodged at the exchange, the 'catalogue' if one prefers. Buyers prepare a list of their needs and the exchange matches them with possible suppliers.

Demand and supply are the same, whether the commodity is potatoes, paper, pipelines or people.

of fish and tyres and rubbery things Some things may never be suitable for online exchanges.

Continental AG, one of the big multinational tyre makers should, in theory, have been concerned when the first item bought by Ford from its online exchange was tyres – from another supplier. But Continental was not in the least worried: which in its way says something about the potential, and the limitations of the marketplace concept.

Its reasoning was simple. While today's vehicles can use tyres from any maker, by and large, only a few months down the road are intelligent 'tyre systems' in which the tyre, and the braking system and chassis suspension are electronically interlinked, with the superior functions of the one totally dependent on the other. And the tyres of one maker will not work on the systems of another.

That in turn means that automakers' systems will have to stay with the manufacturer of the interlinked systems. Such systems, says Continental, are so complicated they cease to become commodities, like today's brakes or tyres, or like power cords for a laptop computer. They cannot be sold or bought based on a single piece, or just a set of specifications lodged online.

It believes that engineered products will be too complex to fit the reverse auction/marketplace concept – and the same considerations apply to aeronautics, railroads, utilities, and semiconductors. In these areas corporate buyers will continue to work closely with a handful of suppliers. It can, and will, still be done online, but not through the marketplace principle.[10]

CASE STUDY

The marketplace revolution has also failed to take hold in the fishing industry, albeit not for the want of trying. Online exchanges such as Gofish.com have now been operating business-to-business links between fishing companies and buyers for two years, but the industry remains entrenched in its traditional trading systems. Fishermen still sell their catch to the processing companies, which use brokers to find wholesale customers who in turn sell to retail outlets, restaurants and hotels. The major reason is that unlike other commodities traded on exchanges, the seafood industry is an amalgamation of a range of businesses that have never had any form of centralized clearing houses.

Gofish and its competitors have tried to break down barriers by offering safeguards about the buyers to the fishermen, including credit checks; they are guaranteeing the transaction by providing insurance and offering immediate payment of up to 80 per cent of the sale price within 48 hours.

But the processing companies say that in an industry built on relationships the online buyer working by e-mail cannot differentiate in quality of the fish it buys: for the moment the processing companies rely on their brokers to make that test. And the brokers are the middlemen who stand to be replaced. Nevertheless, in the summer of 2000, Gofish and its competitors were signing up more and more companies to their exchanges, the gradual change summed up by Wright Gore Jnr. of Western Seafoods who said the worst mistake he could make was 'failing to anticipate' what could be coming. He may have been nostalgic for the past, but he was pragmatic. 'I don't intend for this, or anything else, to run off and leave me if I can help it.'

who will buy?

It is a long time since Nell Gwynne walked the streets around Covent Garden peddling her apples. It is a long time since Covent Garden sold any apples for peddlers to hawk.

Times change. Methods of buying change. In today's world the internet is the buying medium for almost everything, in one form or another.

From online catalogues, through to complex global marketplaces, the aim is still the same: it is to cut costs, eliminate overlap, and add as many competitors to the buying range as possible. In this world supplier portals are nothing more than single sites from which a company can buy anything its employees need to make its operation work.

“times change. Methods of buying change”

By aggregating everything into one electronic operation, where goods can be ordered and paid for on one form, and delivery expedited, they eliminate the drudgery and costs associated with old methods. They eliminate phone calls, multiple payments, multiple form filling. They allow for real-time price comparisons and support multi-currency transactions.

They are the Filofax for the 21st century. They permit inefficiencies to be pushed out of the system just as toothpaste is pushed out of a tube by the pressure of a strategically applied thumb. But just as toothpaste is never fully extracted from the tube, so all inefficiencies will never be eradicated. The internet simply provides tools that will do it better than anything before, and make core savings that are substantial and permanent.

Supply chain consultants say that by the end of 2001 the use of online exchanges will be so ingrained that simply being on the web will cease to be a competitive factor.

"by the end of 2001 simply being on the web will cease to be a competitive factor"

In the meantime the tools are there to reduce errors, fine-tune inventory, adjust manpower and companies truly committed to re-inventing their supply chains will gain the most competitive advantage.[11]

Finance directors and purchasing directors, for whom under The Ecademy '12 Principles' responsibility for this sector lies, need to investigate, learn and educate themselves about the possibilities, as do the project managers and operations directors whose influence also comes to bear.

The end result for their companies will be increased efficiency, better services and cost savings that may be greater than they could expect. Remember organized crime. Or at least Woody Allen's message about it:

> Organized crime in America takes in over 40 billion dollars a year, and spends very little on office supplies.

notes

1 In June 2000 the international firm's website was deactivated because it missed payment on a $35 annual renewal fee for its jpmorgan.com name. Network Solutions, the Virginia-based registrar of internet domain names had reminded it on four separate occasions about the need to renew but 'it appears the contact at JP Morgan was no longer with them or somehow had not been able to respond', according to NS. JP Morgan called it a clerical error. In December 1999 Microsoft's Hotmail system lost service for the same reason. NS reactivated that site after a Tennessee internet consultant paid Microsoft's

$35 renewal fee himself so that he could get access to his e-mail. JP Morgan's site was also reinstated after payment.

2 Interview with David Graham, Buy.co.uk, January 26, 2000.

3 New York Times, June 7, 2000.

4 Chicago Tribune, May 13, 2000.

5 Special article; 'The middle marches towards the internet', Chicago Times, May 13, 2000.

6 Ditto.

7 Ditto.

8 Bernard Stamler, 'Matchmakers for services', New York Times, June 13, 2000.

9 Ditto.

10 Jonathon Yaron, CEO of Enigma Inc, an e-commerce software maker has suggested that the online exchanges will hold a 20 per cent place of the marketplace, not the 90 per cent place that some media analysts have predicted. Thomas Stallkamp, former President of Chrysler and now CEO of MSVX International agrees. He says in the auto industry they will work on 20 per cent or so of the automakers overall purchasing. New York Times, June 7, 2000.

11 Donald Goodwin, Chicago Tribune, July 11, 2000.

11

playing in the junkyard.com: inventory and logistics

“The conduct of war resembles the workings of an intricate machine, with tremendous friction so that combinations which are easily planned on paper can be executed only with great effort. The free will and the mind of the military commander find themselves constantly hampered, and one needs a remarkable strength of mind and soul to overcome this resistance. Many good ideas have perished because of this friction”

Principles of War Application of the Principles in Times of War, Introduction

getting it there without putting it here

Handling costs, inventory costs, just-in-time delivery: we are very good at coming up with business structures that allow our widgets to be kept somewhere else. Now all our back storerooms have become part of the world's warehouse, and it is more efficient because the communications technology is here to do it.

And it can do it – with auctions and digital marketplaces, supplies can be purchased from the lowest bidder and delivered on the day of use. Customers' expectations have quickly caught up with the new situation – the benefits are taken for granted rather than being seen as exceptional service. Delivery is as widely distributed as the FedEx and UPS trucks and planes that constantly circle the globe.

Your customers, your partners and your suppliers are linked to a supply chain through you. In the supplier portal you considered what you had to offer them. Now you need to exploit internal efficiencies. Learn from your understanding of what your buyers want from their relationship with you, and figure out how to apply that to the **inventory and logistics** of your company. It is still part of community development: our previous focus was on external communities, now we are looking inward.

NINTH PRINCIPLE

summary

- inventory and logistics are an internal marketplace
- make your internal logistics systems as easy to operate as your buying systems

IN THE SUMMER OF 2000 Oracle decided that it had hundreds of servers that were surplus to its requirements, in the changing world in which it operated. Where once it had needed 700 servers to carry out its functions it now only needed 100 or so, better and improved models.

In the days BI (before the internet) it would have negotiated the sale of those obsolete machines through a chain of buyers, or stored them in a warehouse and ultimately sold them off as scrap. In the age of the internet it sold them on its own auction site. It had realized that from the angle of the buyer everything is negotiable, especially goods or services which are surplus to requirement, held too long in inventory, obsolete, distressed or overstocked. And it had recognized that from the perspective of the buyer there were new ways of realizing value on items that no longer provide any.

The online auction site is just one of them.

Some companies give the common or garden auction a new internet buzz name, such as Dynamic Pricing, but it still boils down to selling to the highest bidder: because a sold item is money in the bank, and one held in inventory is taking up space, and employee time, and that is money wasted.

“a sold item is money in the bank, and one held in inventory is taking up space, and that is money wasted”

Dynamic Pricing, to use the buzz name, is about pricing an item to be sold at what the customer wants, not what the seller believes it must still be worth. It is about managing raw materials or components for a minimum price, a minimum inventory and managing the life cycle so that even a company as big as Oracle no longer has a warehouse choked with old computers.

In the best of auction situations unwanted stock can now be sold online before it has the chance to be relegated to the warehouse. Computers, for example, can go up for sale immediately they are ready to come off an employee's desk to be replaced with a go-faster model. Many companies still look on the online auction world as a consumer-to-consumer effort: they have seen the headlines about eBay selling the world's only known replica of the 1960s' cartoon car Speed Racer (or stopping the sale of embryos and kidneys).[1]

But the growth in the sector has, hardly noticed by the popular media, occurred faster in the business-to-business and business-to-consumer markets. And it all boils down to moving inventory.

Lastminute.com is arguably the best-known European travel agency online selling last-minute seats on airlines. It is simply selling inventory.

Seats are the inventory of the airlines, and every one it fills with a paying customer, no matter how *little* that customer pays, in the minutes before takeoff is a bonus for the airline operator.

Bums on seats means bucks, after all.

amazon and the junkyard strategy

Critics have accused Jeff Bezos, the charismatic head of Amazon.com, of being many things: short sighted, ill informed, overly ambitious and failing to understand that business has to be based on profits. But no one has ever openly accused him in print of being stupid. (Although it has to be said that by the middle of 2000 he was being accused of refusing to face reality, and of purveying in-your-face confidence while leading the company towards forecast bankruptcy.)[2]

All of which made Amazon's decision – which developed over a period of months from the end of 1999 – to go into the online auction business highly interesting.

Amazon's aim is to become the one-stop site for everyone to do everything, which means an online auction site was inevitable. But it is what developed with the site that has relevance in the business world – like others it became in part what Forbes Magazine was to call a 'dumping ground for returned, damaged, discontinued and overstocked goods'.

> "bums on seats means bucks, after all"

It said the 'junkyard approach' had become part of Amazon's corporate strategy – a paradox given the way that Amazon has consistently touted the quality of its brand.

But its comments were based on marketplace reality: Amazon went late into the auction game, in early 1999, and gradually carved its niche in the area that had somehow mostly passed by eBay, with its person-to-person bias. (In 1998 more than 90 per cent of all sales on eBay were consumer to consumer.)

Its auction site became a cyber version of what the British know as the rag and bone man, à la Steptoe and Son, translocated to the USA as Sanford and Son. Amazon, in the early part of 2000, had provided one of the major homes on the internet for unwanted and unsold goods, and its officials began to spread the gospel that it was better able to liquidate products than were traditional offline liquidators.

In the summer it began to pilot more of such relationships with branded merchants, building on an early alliance it had made with companies such as Service Merchandise, and Gear.com, both featured on its site.

According to Amazon at this time electronic and kitchen products which could not be returned to manufacturers by retailers, after they had been sent to them by irate consumers, or which were simply unsold, outdated inventory, were selling on its web auction site at between 20 per cent to 80 per cent of retail prices, compared with the 20 to 60 per cent of cost recorded by traditional methods.

Amazon then took 5 per cent in sales commission.

The financial attraction of this model was clear, and traditional liquidators have been quick to move into the online auction area. Redtagoutlet.com, a Minneapolis company, was among the pioneers – it evolved from a traditional liquidator and one of its first deals was to auction the closing-down stock of Make Us An Offer, which had decided to go into a new business as a technology provider.

Robert Israel, the CEO of Make Us An Offer, said later the online auctioneer 'served as our cleaner outers'.

Methods of managing an inventory, inventory logistics, are an integral part of a business plan, and in today's world the issue of liquidation as a means of inventory reduction has gained a new twist in the shape of the online auctions. They may not be regarded as part of a traditional concept of the supply chain – but they should clearly be an intrinsic part of an e-commerce armoury.

do it yourself – well, almost Closeouts, sales of damaged goods and disposal of overstocked inventory comprise a $10 billion segment of the homebuilding and refurbishment industry. They also represent a huge problem for manufacturers who need to move these products quickly, and who, frankly, do not want to resort to a liquidator.

That was where Buildscape saw its niche. It envisaged a site where building contractors and individual consumers could shop, investigate, and interact – and move the materials that otherwise would go at giveaway prices through the traditional liquidation channels.

Since it was without in-house expertise Buildscape bought a turnkey solution from an online auction solutions provider and, using a clearing-house model, began to host auctions featuring everything from screwdrivers and forklifts to plywood and roofing shingles.[3]

The result was a win for the industry and everyone else. Manufacturers earned profits where they used to take losses; contractors and consumers were able to choose from a greater variety of products at an attractive cost savings; Buildscape augmented its e-commerce business with a successful new auction strategy.

> “branded auctions for inventory moving began to take off in late 1999”

Branded auctions of this nature for inventory moving began to take off in late 1999 and are now an established online industry, serving both the online and off-line business sector. They combine the idea of inventory control and management, with bottom-line boost – and the building of a community of regular users, which is an imperative in a web strategy. But they also build brand equity, developing loyal customers who come back for the type of goods that the sites sell and the services they provide.

And they provide it at internet speed.

Where once a manufacturer, wholesaler or retailer might have to wait weeks or months for a full-scale liquidation sale to realize a return on materials that simply took up warehouse space, he is now able to post the items online, stipulate a time limit on bids, or a set price, and know that within a matter of days the surplus has been taken off the company's hands. For other companies, owning their own auction site has the added advantage of developing a new community, a new database of bidders and clients, and providing added value in a tool that can be used in other marketing sectors.

three stages of life

Among the worst of the non-words that e-commerce has spawned is 'disintermediation'. It is a polite term for cutting out sales forces, distributors, wholesalers and buyers. And it is where the online auction comes into its own.

The internet cannot store and pack goods, it cannot deliver them. But it can drive down prices by allowing suppliers to bid against each other, as in the online marketplace scenario of the previous chapter, and it can enhance profits by getting rid of unwanted inventory, and allowing inventory to be managed through the auction system.

It can 'disintermediate' the intermediaries.

It is a piece of the jigsaw that fits into the picture of the different stages in the life cycle of any commodity.

The beginning of the life cycle is when a product or service is first released. At this stage there are several possibilities: it can founder, it can succeed mildly, or it can succeed beyond expectations, and catch the manufacturer or company making the service offer unable to produce sufficient to satisfy the market demand.

This is the time when traditional retailers make big promotions and charge equally big premiums. But in the online auction world this still applies – when a model first emerges it is becoming the norm for someone to obtain supplies and put them up for sale to the highest bidder while stocks are scarce.

BMW did this in the USA in 1999, offering the first model of its about-to-be-released SUV for auction for charity – it raised more than three times the estimated street price and even when the model was released it commanded a premium, online and off.

In June 2000 while Palm was struggling to meet demand for its handheld computers because of a shortage of components, customers were turning to eBay and other auction sites and paying well above retail prices for new and slightly used units.[4]

Palm said it was making and shipping more of the products at the time than it had ever made or shipped before, but could not keep up with demand because of the component shortages. This underscores the point that using an online auction is not just about the disposing of inventory, or only about reducing risk. It is equally about making money in times when there is shortage of certain products – as opposed to foolishly giving them away at the normal price when people are prepared to pay a premium.

“an online auction is not just about the disposing of inventory.”

(Oracle used a twist even on this theme in July 2000. It put the first ten of its new internet computers (NICs) on the Amazon.com auction site, with a certificate of authenticity signed by CEO, Larry Ellison, two weeks before it was due to release them for $199 without a monitor. Within days they were attracting bids of $550 – which meant nothing in financial terms to Oracle but was an indicator to its marketing department of the demand that it could anticipate on general release. By the time the auction finished on July 10 the price had risen to $1,650 – although one man who bought eight admitted he had done so because of Ellison's signature.)

At the middle of the life cycle, a manufacturer is forced to use other tactics to generate volume – a sale, or a promotion. This too occurs online.

CASE STUDY

General Motors used the internet extensively in 2000 to offer promotional discounts for its popular midsize models in the USA. It offered between $200 and $1,000 on some vehicles in a month-long promotion on a new site called GM Ticket to Ride, co-ordinating the promotion with advertising off-line in national magazines and on television, and online with American Online.[5]

Like many automakers worldwide, General Motors has struggled to streamline an inefficient distribution system for its products and perfect a system where the most popular cars arrive at the retailers' showrooms at the peak of the demand. And the result is auto dealers' lots overflowing with expensive inventory, and vehicles that have to be discounted to ease the glut. That was where the promotion, only available online, came in.

GM Vice-President, John Middlebrook, said that the beauty of this system on the internet was that it 'gives us flexibility. We can vary and change the discounts depending on market conditions. We know what is going on every minute every day and can adjust accordingly.'[6] It was, he admitted, a 'great learning experience'.

At the end of a life cycle, the manufacturer, the wholesaler, or the retailer who has bought too much, has to ask how he gets rid of the last amount of inventory. In the atomic world car dealers and manufacturers have learned it is easy to manage the life cycle because they know that everyone likes to pay less, and particular clients would rather use their finance loan to trade their four-year-old BMW for a two-year-old BMW for £250 a month than for £350. But at the same time there is always a buyer in his rented property who still wants the image and is happy to take a six-year-old BMW for £50 a month.

So it can target the once-every-two years' buyer with a better offer, knowing it can offload its inventory of new materials to him or her, while then passing on the older vehicle down the market chain, realizing a ready sale at most stages as long as the price is right.

In the meantime, for the rest of business, there is inventory control.

In the ultimate cyber business world, however, inventory will disappear, as retailers and manufacturers begin to exploit the art of data mining, for profiles which will match their production to the demand they can fairly confidently predict will occur.

> “the inventory minimal operation is the wider retail world of the future”

Electrical wholesalers and retailers will know when a customer is moving house, through their links to the realtors and the mortgage lenders, and they will be able to contact potential buyers who will probably need a new fridge, a new freezer, a new microwave, a new cooker, a new television, a new washing machine and a new dryer for the new home.

They would already do it if they had any way of knowing about potential movements – but in the present system they do not know until a customer walks into the store and says he or she has moved home and needs whatever it is. For the householder the advantages are that the goods are ready to be installed in the new home on the day of moving (or the day after, or before, if it is more convenient) instead of waiting for weeks for delivery and connection: and the probability of a special price for such a bundle of ordered items.

The clear gain for the wholesaler/retailer is being able to supply a bundle of goods, and make them or import them almost to order, the way that Dell has for years made and delivered only to order over the internet.

The inventory minimal operation is the wider retail world of the future. Until then there are off-line liquidators and online auctions.

no end to the variety

There are numerous web services that cater for business-to-business auction needs and often specialize in the type of goods sold, from industrial and laboratory equipment, through to computers and electronic parts – any part of the business spectrum.

One online auctioneer deals only in livestock, another auctions baseballs, dozens are devoted to memorabilia. There are auction sites for stamp collectors, coin collectors, and even skateboards.

And like all good operations on the internet the system that has developed is simple.

Cyber auctions work on the basis of a bidder online tapping in his bid on the keyboard. The bid is instantly recognized at the auction end, compared to other incoming bids and a response is generated. There are official closing times for online auctions, but in general terms an electronic gavel ‘comes down’ if there has been no bid for around two minutes. Some auctions last an hour, some up to a week or more.

And, in the end, the highest bidder wins.

In the reverse auction mode, used extensively for selling last-minute inventory in airplanes, on car rental lots and in hotels to consumers, pioneered by Priceline.com, the would-be customer types in how much he or she is prepared to pay for an item, and the site itself puts that bid to the various companies. Those that match it are linked to the buyer.

Whichever model – and there are others – the aim is always the same: inventory control. But it is only one of many ways of controlling the inventory that are available to the online company.

In all of them the system should be used either as an overall strategy or as a method of reducing stock, when it is aged or over-bought, or simply in the wrong location.[7]

> “cyber auctions work on the basis of a bidder online tapping in his bid on the keyboard”

Inventory logistics are the responsibility, in this world, of the operations, sales and finance directors, working with suggestions from the marketing director (who will help maintain overall company image) and the purchasing director, who will have to control the supply of information on purchasing trends and future opportunities.

But never, before the internet, have they had such an arsenal of possibilities.

notes

1 In June 2000 Jim Rocknowski, of Speed Racer Enterprises put a replica of the two-door roadster copied from the 1960s' cartoon character, for sale on eBay's site. The rocket-like car was a Japanese cartoon depicting the adventures of a teenager who battled evil around the world. It had a fan base of more than 50 million by the time it was discontinued in 1967. The replica was built for Child Safety Network, an organization promoting child safety and protection issues across the USA.

2 Seattle Times, July 3, 2000. Two weeks after Amazon's stock was sent crashing by an analyst's report on its creditworthiness, the Seattle Times said that until then Jeff Bezos'

'arrogance had been on a fast track to reality', but that six months after being named as Time's Man of The Year (1999) his halo had gone and that Amazon was looking more and more like a concept stock such as Discovery Zone, and Planet Hollywood – all of which took on a lot of debt and ultimately had to file for bankruptcy.

3 It used a product from OpenSite, a North Carolina company with international reach, which was the first to offer packaged online auction applications to the business market.

4 Los Angeles Times, June 23, 2000. It said that bids for low end Palm IIIes which had a $149 retail price at the time, had been topping $200 in online auctions, while the Palm V had been gaining bids above its $329 suggested price.

5 It also used online incentives such as sweepstakes. In one in June 2000 it was offering the winner a chance to play golf with Tiger Woods, in others a trip to the upcoming summer Olympics in Australia.

6 CNet, June 3, 2000.

7 General Motors also uses the internet to determine how to shift models that are not selling in one part of the country to another region where they may be hot. If a dealer in California cannot unload its Cavaliers in the height of summer, GM uses the feedback on the site to target California with special offers to make them more attractive. It leaves the price untouched in other regions. And when sales pick up, such as those of four-wheel drive vehicles in the Rockies in winter, it can eliminate the incentive.

12

a valuable economic factor: the internet as ideal selling mechanism

"A powerful emotion must stimulate the great ability of a military leader. Open your heart to such emotion. Be audacious and cunning in your plans, firm and persevering in their executions, determined to find a glorious end, and fate will crown your youthful brow with a shining glory"

Principles of War
Applications of the Principles

if you build it they will come... Maybe. Certainly that was true when the cyber marketplace was a big empty field, then anything new was something to go and look at. Like modern architects vying to build the most interesting building, websites went up with flashy or subversive design. Any content was interesting, because all sites were somehow 'trials' of what was to come in the future.

Now we have grown bored. Or, if you prefer, we have matured into web sophisticates who demand that the on-line experience somehow matches or exceeds the live one. And the argument isn't what we were told it would be – that all would rely on the security issues surrounding on-line payments – it is about the buyer's experience.

power to the people Music, media, tickets – non-tactile products, things that you don't need to touch to enjoy – are clearly the first wave of consumer web purchases. Many companies – especially in the automotive industry – are discovering that the web is becoming an increasingly important part of the purchase process, but that the actual purchase is still reserved for the retail outlet. This is integration. E-business is ceasing to be something discrete, it is melding with all the existing business processes.

So what can the new communications technology of the internet do for you as a selling mechanism ? Well, for one thing your rolodex has suddenly become much, much bigger. You now have the power to communicate with people on a one-to-one basis via electronic means.

TENTH PRINCIPLE

You might think that the problem is finding something to say, but in fact the less you say the better. The most successful communities on the web are not those that push content out endlessly to their members from some central source, but those that encourage their members to speak among themselves.

There was been a sort of hub-and-spoke idea of online selling, which pictured the company at the centre, and the buyers out there at the end of the spokes. The customers would slowly circle the hub, passing through different points of the sales cycle, guided by some predictable set of electronic conversations.

But that isn't how it has turned out at all. In fact, the web is a better place for people to decide *not* to buy a particular product, than to decide to buy it. Imagine that you want to buy a car, you would go to a user group and see what people say about various different models. The ones with really lousy feedback could be crossed off the shortlist right away, but you would still want to test drive the good ones.

summary

- if you build it, they might not come
- some products are ideally suited to sale over the internet
- customers like to interact with other customers
- use the internet appropriately – as part of the sales *process*

CASE STUDY

LINDA KATZ SOMEHOW managed, along the road, to get herself re-christened. She became known around the world as the Tumbleweed Lady.

In late 1997 Ms Katz, of Garden City, Kansas, wanted to build a website. A 'this is my dog, this is my cat' affair that would be folksy but not too boring. So she rounded up a bunch of nieces and nephews, dressed them in hard hats, borrowed a backhoe and some other construction equipment from a friend and took photographs of what she thought she would call the 'staff' of Prairie Tumbleweed Farm, harvesting their 'organically grown, hand selected tumbleweeds.'

Why not?

The yellow grey weeds that blow across the heart of the USA were certainly folksy – and everybody around the world knew them through a million Westerns, blowing down Main Street while the white-hatted hero prepared to go out into the stillness and meet his black-hatted foe.

The weeds, also known as Russian Thistles, bounce around Kansas like lost balloons, careening through the pastures and fields and piling up against barbed wire fences along the roads like creatures in a Stephen King novel.

So she put them on her website and called it – naturally enough – www.tumbleweedfarm.com and sat back waiting for the laughter from her friends.

What she got was a call from a woman in New Jersey ordering two of the organically produced tumbleweeds for a wedding reception.

She went out into her garden, picked up a couple, boxed them and shipped them and had a chuckle to herself. But the joke was on her because the orders never stopped coming.

Since then the Tumbleweed Lady has had her weeds shipped to buyers in Scotland, Singapore, and Scandinavia and had them on display in Bloomingdale's department store. They have appeared in children's television shows, and in mid-2000 starred in a US public television series highlighting the natural beauties of America.

Now, says Ms Katz, 'If you see a commercial on television with a tumbleweed in it, it's usually one of ours.'

She and a friend still go out and round up tumbleweeds, mostly close to the Sunflower Electric Generating plant on the edge of Garden City, where the tumbleweeds are nicely well rounded, and piled up in gullies near the fences.

Nowadays she has branched out into T-shirts with tumbling tumbleweeds which are hot on college campuses and has brought in other family members who are listed company officials getting a share of the profits. In 1999 she made $20,000 selling a product picked up for nothing.

The purpose of this anecdote is not to sell more tumbleweeds for Ms Katz, who is doing nicely anyway: rather to demonstrate that in an internet world global selling of anything is only as far away as the consumer demand. All it takes are audacious plans, and perseverance in their execution as von Clausewitz advised his pupil. The internet is potentially an ideal selling mechanism.

And for most people or companies, a little knowledge of the latest marketing tools.

salesman's dream, salesman's nightmare

The internet has no unions. It has no night and day and it has no statutory trading restrictions. It is a 24-hours-a-day, seven-days-a-week, 365-days-a-year, non-stop trading community unfettered by the human, governmental, or space restrictions that have always hobbled traditional methods of selling. And in a leap year it works the full 366 days around the clock.

It is a market where someone is always open, someone is always buying.

In this salesman's dream however, many things can go wrong. If goods are promised and not delivered, the internet customer will not accept excuses, he or she will go elsewhere. If the website is difficult to understand or navigate, the browser will go elsewhere. If the site is overloaded with graphics and slow to load onto the screen, a potential buyer will disengage. Look at Boo.com.

“in an internet world global selling of anything is only as far away as the consumer demand”

And just as somewhere, all the time, someone is buying, the e-business has to keep in mind that somewhere, a competitor is always selling. That is the salesman's nightmare.

It should go without saying that e-merchants must create a website that encourages people to visit, to buy. It must delight them with a great experience so they return to buy again and again.

And it is the responsibility of every company's sales and marketing directors to make sure the criteria are met, listening to project managers, and finance and operations directors to ensure the decisions are in line with the company's long- and short-term plans to buy goods and collect payment.

The web has supplied the merchant with an undreamt of arsenal of tools ranging from the so-called 'call me software' (which those in the business prefer to call customer support tools) to web-authoring technology allowing companies to build their own sites, web databases, front-end and back-end e-commerce suites.

> "the internet has no unions. It has no night and day and it has no statutory trading restrictions"

Throw in affiliation software, multimedia graphic design software, content publishing and search engines, which link a company site to the major search engines, and there are enough technical terms to delight a webmaster's heart and push a CEO into head-holding despair.

As it happens Linda Katz had very few of these. She did not even know they existed. She went ahead and built her site with just a little basic knowledge, then sought advice from her local ISP on how to get a domain name and the first orders came by happenstance. Now she lists on search engines, using those as selling aids, but little more.

Which only highlights the possibilities available for a company with resources to spare, and the knowledge of how to use them.

By the same token, of course, she may not have been an entrepreneur at all. Just an unknown (and unknowing) artist. Because as Frank Zappa said, 'Art is making something out of nothing and then selling it.'

something for nothing

Getting something for nothing is at the heart of the internet ethos, as many companies which have gone online and tried to charge for their content have found. But in a seller's world, offering something for nothing can be a direct way to increased sales. In 1997 Phoneme made its debut online with a selling tool which is uniquely simple in concept, hideously complicated in flawless execution – but which provides a consumer with something for nothing… a direct link into a business he wants to buy from, no matter where it is located in the world.

Phoneme calls itself a service, not a product. This is the way it works. A UK consumer logs onto its site. He or she has seen an ad on the net late in the evening or on television about a pair of Nike shoes and wants to know if they are for baseball or running and wants to know now. The local stores are long since closed, as are Nike's offices in the UK. The website doesn't say. And with e-mails notoriously inefficient in response times, and no 0-800 facilities available from Britain to the USA he (or she) does not want to pay hard cash for an expensive transatlantic phone call.

Phoneme invites him to enter his own number, and the number of whomsoever he is contacting. The company he has called will return the call, using any phone number for the return, fixed line or mobile. It says that before the customer-in-waiting has clicked on the mouse to close down the phone will ring, and it will be someone from Nike answering the call.[1]

“offering something for nothing can be a direct way to increased sales”

Phoneme has programmed the Nike call centre number and links to it over the net: it feeds the call-back number onto the Nike server and that is it, in simplistic terms. The call-back request is picked up by a 24-hour Nike call centre, and the return phone call is made.

By bringing the two calls together it is, in a sense, conferencing across the internet. The advantage for the consumer is that it is a free call. And when the call is returned the consumer is talking to a real person at the end of a line, and that helps break down the next fear barrier – that of entering a credit card number to buy the pair of shoes.

The benefit for Nike is a reduction in the actual cost of the sale – because Phoneme is not a telecommunications company Nike does not have to pay anyone for the call either, and it knows that the person it is calling is a definite interest lead.

Phoneme's service started in the back bedroom of the London home of Damon Oldcorn: then his team managed to get Compaq, Dell, Hewlett Packard, NatWest bank and others on board, and the rest is history.

It is not unique – in the way of the internet it now has other competitors big and small, and all offer a way to sell that before the internet age was too expensive to be possible, but produces real return on investment.

It is however, a prime example of the selling tools that are available and are unique to the web.

let there be music

There are many others, most of them to do with the visible face of an e-company, the website.

> "a website cannot just be a pretty face"

The face is the first thing a customer will see, and which provides the initial turn-on or turn-off. Even in a business-to-business operation the visual face that a company presents can be crucial to creating that first image. But a website cannot just be a pretty face: like anything else it has to have something beneath the skin.

CASE STUDY

In January 2000 Octane Music, a UK internet music company, decided it wanted an internet portal designed and built for music delivery, connected to its other operations, and it wanted it up and running in less than two months.

Like Vivendi's Jean-Claude Messier, Octane's founder, Roger Press, believes that music and the internet were a business match made in heaven. His mantra is that: 'Where there is a chip, there will be music.'

Press, a former music industry executive, said he was not satisfied to offer 'just another' music retail site on the web with 24/7 access to a global clientele. He wanted to: 'free the world from the constraints of physical music collections:

Wherever you are, we want to deliver your favourite music onto your desktop, into your car, even to your cellphone in real time.'

The hyperbole is fairly normal in the internet environment, but Octane did own an extensive library of jazz recordings and a catalogue of classic music. Its portal site, Cicada, could use that collection to blend e-commerce with streaming audio, allow customers to download MP3 files, and personalize and customize the making of CDs.

The consulting company he hired decided to go for a relatively new off-the-shelf product that claimed it would provide a world solution under tight deadlines.[2] (Octane's was actually its test bed.)

The technology would provide extensive integration with existing systems, personalization and up-to-date retail features as well as cross-marketing and reporting. Developing a proprietary solution was not a viable option because the test site had to go live after only six weeks.

The product handled common functions such as sophisticated product catalogues, shopping baskets and electronic payments, but also provided a site face (the graphical user interface (GUI)) with drag-and-drop features that would make it easy to create and edit business flows while the site was still in development, and would allow Octane to change and modify business flows as market demands changed and required adaptation of the site's functionality.

It handled the music download department with ease and accepted payments through a secure system integrated with a British high street bank.

The solutions-providing company gave the training that Octane's staff needed on the system, and helped customize it to the music site's demands. And it did it within the six-week deadline, taking into account the development that everyone knew would be needed after the shakedown period following the launch.

Companies such as Intershop – which provided Octane's solution – identify themselves as sell-side operators.[3] And increasingly they are working hand in hand with the procurement experts, to provide total sites. Sites that go beyond the face, and provide a tool which sells, not just attracts.

build, integrate, promote

Microsoft, now toppled from its throne as the world's biggest company, but still the world leader in software for personal and business computing, believes in a three-word strategy for e-commerce – build, integrate, promote.[4]

The build part of the strategy is about helping companies build web presence. It has a suite of products for that.

The integrate part is about taking that website and integrating it with a company's existing legacy or heritage systems and supplier and customers' systems. It has products for that, too.

The promote part is about the role of the portal. The company has built a website, integrated it with suppliers, and then begins the process of promoting it to the world and opening for electronic commerce.

And naturally it has products for that, also built on a three-word slogan.[5]

This time the words are engage, transact, analyze.

The engage part is about designing and building websites that help the client company engage with the customer, without ever having to talk with them. This area is about personalization, which we look at in the final chapter.

The transact part is about the ability to conduct online transactions in a secure and authenticated manner, which we have already dealt with.

The analyze part is about discovering answers to questions such as, 'How often did I sell product x from page 32 of my website during the month of March between the hours of 10 and 12?'

This is so-called 'rich analysis' of website traffic – and it should never be more than just 3 or 4 clicks away. These are the data that the internet can provide to a company which allows it to analyze its selling, to target those areas which are working well and selling properly, and ask the right questions about those that are not, before it decides to eliminate them.

It is the kind of analysis which, in the past, companies have paid outsiders to perform, and which now can be incorporated into the building of their web operation, for in-house investigation, by any of the companies, like Microsoft, that have developed ways for any firm, especially a small e-commerce store to get onto the internet with least hassle.

Its MSN portal is sometimes reported as number one or number two in the UK for online service. It created one of the more popular portals in Europe, and so successful has it been at targeting the consumer, it had 18,000 public communities in the first eight weeks after introducing its MSN Web Communities section and 3 million users in two months when it introduced its MSN Messenger Service.[6]

But it also has a section called bCentral, aimed at the small business customer. It allows businesses to get online by building a store very simply themselves or getting a partner to do it for them. It connects it to its link exchange, which has 75 per cent coverage of the websites on the internet.

The MSN service is far from unique – all the portals now have store-building sites aimed squarely at the small business sector, all offering various functions that others may not have.

The one thing they have in common is that they provide a fast and easy way for a company to get into the physical business of selling online.

They provide another tool in the selling process.

How well the small business uses that tool is a matter of how well it has applied all of the other underlying principles that must be integrated to improve the chances of success.

can I do you now sir?

It takes a long memory, but back in the days of World War II, when the radio was the only means of entertainment, there was a British show called 'Itma' ('It's that Man Again') which had as one of its regular segments the entry of a cleaning lady wanting to tidy up a room, who would say to the lead, 'Can I do you now sir?'

Cleaning was the intention. Permission was the ingredient she required.

Permission marketing antecedes the internet by generations: newspapers have used their subscription list, with permission to send regular readers offers of commercial items, book clubs have permission to send their customers new books every month. At the lowest level, someone once said, permission is at the heart of the electricity delivery system – because a customer gives the power company permission to sell him electricity every time he switches on a light.

On the internet, permission marketing is just another tool in the armoury of the selling company.

> “on the internet, permission marketing is just another tool in the armoury of the selling company”

It starts the instant anyone provides an e-mail address, as it does with a customer giving a physical address to his off-line bank.

In the e-business world e-mail targeting is now widely used, and abused, although in its finest form, used in connection with tracking software it can be the heart to personalization which is one of the keys to internet business. But in the time since e-commerce began to spread across the world outside the USA (in 1999) the marketplace for this type of selling has changed. The consumer has become aware of e-mail selling and shies away from it.

The low-lying fruit has gone.

Into this space now have stepped companies such as ChooseYourMail, which ask consumers to specify not just what marketing e-mails they are prepared to accept, but how often they will accept, and how long they think their interest may continue. It also sends all marketing material in uniform format, using HTML, and only five kilobytes long, which avoids the anger of the anti-spam activists, and placates the customer.[7]

If e-mail permission marketing is done correctly, with the company involved disclosing what it is doing for itself, or for a client business, and if it ensures privacy then consumers will sign up for marketing e-mail, and will read and respond more readily to what they get. Which in the end is what the businessman wants.

The measure of the effectiveness of such a selling tool is not how many mailings are sent out, or the number of names on a vendor's selling list, but the number of responses that are returned. Which is why some of the new marketing companies in this field try to keep response rates high and churn rates low, by refusing clients it believes may not be suitable.

> “in the e-business world e-mail targeting is widely used, and abused”

Permission marketing through this route is already used by advertising agencies for clients such as Kraft Foods and Blockbuster Video. They use permission marketing databases with details on everyone mailed, including their rate of response to past mailings.[8]

According to Deborah Herst, the Midwest regional director of Bluestreak.com, an e-mail marketing company in Rhode Island, the cost of acquiring a customer this way can be a quarter of what it might take with another medium. In mid-2000 the estimated cost of prospecting a customer for e-mail permission marketing in the USA was reportedly $20. The cost of retaining that customer was $1.[9]

buy another bottle from the travelling man

Pop singer Cher once had a hit song called 'Gypsies, Tramps, and Thieves'. It was all about her daddy who was a travelling medicine man, peddling his cure-all elixir from his travelling wagon, and moving from town to town just ahead of the tar and feathers, as far as one can gather. For him the only selling tools available were fast patter and a gaudily decorated wagon – and the only accessory he needed was a pair of sturdy horses to get him out of town before anyone drank his product.

> "the internet is the very antithesis of the travelling salesman"

The internet is the very antithesis of the travelling salesman. He went to the world. Today the world comes to him, or the company that employs him. But selling is still the name of the game, and an arsenal of good tools is still an aid to doing it.

And no one has invented virtual tar and feathers.

Not yet anyway.

notes

1 Interview with Damon Oldcorn, PhoneMe, January 2, 2000.

2 PriceWaterhouse Coopers.

3 Intershop eFinity. Intershop Communications Inc. is one of the world's leading providers of sell-side electronic commerce software for complete business-to-business and business-to-consumer solutions. Customers include many of the world's largest telecommunications companies such as Deutsche Telekom, France Telecom, Bell South, Swisscom, BCE Energis, MindSpring, PSINet and TicketMaster Online-CitySearch. It has divided its product sets into two product lines to support different business models – selling direct, selling indirect, enabling merchants and marketplaces. Intershop eFinity is

a next generation XML and Java-based product released in October 1999 designed to allow clients to take orders from new web devices such as mobile phones and PDAs.

4 Based in Redmond, Washington, and with 35,000 employees across the world, Microsoft generated net revenues of $20 billion and net income of $8 billion in 1999 – a growth of 73 per cent over the previous 12 months. Over 40 per cent of its employees work in research and development and another 45 per cent in sales and support and the average reported age of its employees is 34.

5 John Noakes, Microsoft, January 13, 2000.

6 Microsoft's core internet engine product is Commerce Server, running on IIS.

7 Dana Blake Horn, Chicago Tribune, July 11, 2000.

8 Ditto.

9 Ian Oxman, President of ChooseYourMail.com, Chicago Tribune, July 11, 2000

13

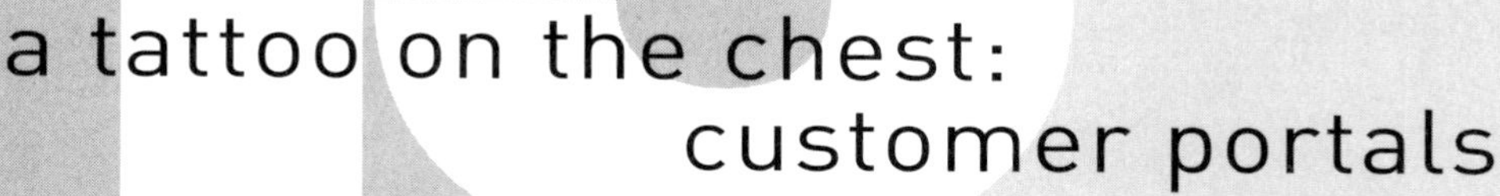

a tattoo on the chest: customer portals

“Warfare has three main objectives:
(a) to conquer and destroy the armed power of the enemy;
(b) to take possession of his material and other sources of strength; and
(c) to gain public opinion.
Public opinion is won through great victories and the occupation of the enemy's capital”

Principles of War
Strategy: General Principles 1 and 4

"I wouldn't want to join any club that would have me as a member."

Groucho Marx

If you want to sell on-line you need a compelling product, better pricing than your competitors, and a willingness to invest and reinvest in evolving an online strategy which treats customers as a community – the creation of customer portals.

ELEVENTH PRINCIPLE

Seth Godin, in his book *Permission Marketing*, identifies many of the things that are important for creating lasting relationships with customers. Most important is the idea that customers are far more likely to respond to company information if they feel that they have somehow asked for it. But that still assumes a hub-and-spoke relationship between the customer audience and the company. We are still trying to slide purchasers down a prescribed purchasing path by building confidence based on a manipulated sense of permission.

from tribalism to cultishness

Others talk of binding people into a sense of community or tribalism, so that we are all Amazonians or Yahooligans. We may be, except we rarely speak to one another in the context of being Amazonians. We talk as colleagues, or friends, or as part of some other relationship, but almost never as Amazonians.

Cults have a method of recruitment that relies upon being not sold but somehow happened upon. You meet someone on the platform of a train station who strikes up a friendship, seemingly with no intention, but there is an insidious underlying agenda. This kind of technique has been taken up by modern methods of 'clever internet marketing', but we cannot assume that the market won't get wise. There is a post-modern media theory that basically says we are all cynical towards manipulative techniques, even if we remain coerced on occasion. We find it more and more difficult to feel good about our transactions, so we move towards insular, non-community based entertainments and activities, such as TV and video games, rather than interact in a world which appears ever friendlier but in fact becomes ever more manipulative.

That is what we need to be avoid. We need to create communities, where people can trust one another, where participation isn't rewarded by being flogged a whole variety of new products. What makes Yahoo! interesting is that they rarely ask for any money, even though they provide you with a whole range of services. Thus it has become the benchmark – it is now what we expect.

We go to Amazon because we want to buy a book. There is some semblance of community book reviews and suggestions. But visits are task oriented, not social. So how do you create a social network? By encouraging conversations between people – not hub-to-spoke conversations, but conversations between spokes. Use the information you learn to refine your offering to the market.

summary

- have good products, competitive prices and invest in community building
- try not to be slick and manipulative
- encourage genuine social interaction between your customers
- don't constantly try to foist yourself on your customers

AN INDIANA UNIVERSITY PROFESSOR is once reputed to have said about Harley Davidson owners, 'If you can persuade your customers to tattoo your name on their chests, they probably will not switch brands.'

It was a relevant point: Harley Davidson is arguably the finest example in the world today of establishing an aura about a brand, allowing the company to sell old technology and do it more profitably than those manufacturers who have poured billions of dollars into their research and development divisions.[1]

But it has always been a basic principle of business that the way for a company to get ahead is to give people what they want.

> "it has always been a basic principle of business that the way for a company to get ahead is to give people what they want"

Harley Davidson just tapped a nostalgic niche and found money in it, giving the customers what they want, and establishing a customer portal.

The age of e-commerce has added a few extra gorillas to the basic premise in the shape of 'when they want it, where they want it, and how they want it', but the essence remains the same.

In the real world it was to some extent what made Wal-Mart the most successful retailing company in history, with Sam Walton pursuing his idea that if everything were put under one roof, at a price people could afford, they would come to his stores and buy.

Wal-Mart lost its way with the dawn of the internet age but it realized this in 1999 and tried to claw its way back in – more successfully through its British purchase of the Asda supermarket chain than through its efforts back on home territory in the USA. By the time Wal-Mart moved online the bulk e-tailing territory had already been largely captured by the portals – Yahoo!, Microsoft's MSN, AOL, Excite (and its AtHome partner in the USA), Amazon.com and so on.

And the Battle of the Portals was over before Wal-Mart caught up with the rearguard. The portals had moved on, and they continue to move on, morphing as they go from echoes of Sam Walton's mega-markets into the new global public utilities.[2]

Wal-Mart entered the fray still thinking of portals as just another !distribution channel. Yahoo! and Amazon had already evolved into the new information masters.

Nevertheless, customer portals remain an essential part of the e-business process, inextricably linked with the idea of building a 'community'.

When signing up to a portal members must register, preferably in as uncomplicated a way as possible. But from that registration the portal, the new information master, can build up a demographic record collated in a database that develops into a valuable asset for the business to tempt advertisers and e-merchants. Not only that, it allows the company to begin to plan its sales targeting with much clearer aims, and improved chances of success. It is, to refer back to an earlier chapter, the way it knows how to schedule reminders to customers if something is available which might interest them, when their purchased products might need replacing, or at the very least servicing.

It is the key to the 21st century marketing vault.

Logging onto a portal on the internet is like entering a hypermarket door. On one side are the services – banking, insurance, financial services such as stock market quotes, health advice, travel services, and education. On the other side are the equivalent of the cafes and eateries – the entertainment sites, just for listening to music and watching videos, reading the news, tracing the family history. Straight ahead are shops, and the cyber shelves loaded with everything available in the real world and much more, from groceries through to clothing, books through to CDs, videos and white goods. At the back are the auction sites, offering access to anything the heart desires and the pocket can afford.

Under each generic category (consider them to be the generic malls) are hundreds, if not thousands, of subcategories – the cyber shops – to investigate and explore.

No human hand has ever built such a shopping city in bricks and mortar, glass, wood, polycarbonates and steel.

By following a hierarchical route, any browser can hyperlink to millions of websites, windowshopping for products, services or information, with a 'guide' to help find the shortest path through the labyrinth in the form of search engine technology.

“the aim of Yahoo!, Amazon and others, has been to create shopping nirvana”

At the end of it all lies the checkout – where a customer can buy anything he or she may have picked up in a shopping cart along the journey, but equipped with an equally convenient side aisle where a click of the mouse takes him or her back out… and if the mood is right into another, different, cybertropolis.

The aim of Yahoo!, Amazon and others, has been to create shopping nirvana.

A virtual shopper's paradise which no one will ever leave for another place no matter whether they arrived by personal computer, interactive television, mobile phone, bank ATM or whatever may have emerged since this was written.

The key lies in capturing the customer and no one has encapsulated it better than Amazon.com's Jeff Bezos with his throwaway line that has become the most quoted piece of advice to the new business generation – 'Be a community builder, be a facilitator and be a networker'.

the reach versus revenue balance

Up to the stock market fall of spring 2000 much of the new e-business world followed the belief of Bezos that profits were for next year, like Jerusalem.

Amazon was the most headlined of the dot coms that preached that building the brand was the most important thing in the infancy of the internet, and that profits would come when they would come.

But it was not alone in that attitude.

CASE STUDY

Microsoft's MSN financed its operation in part with payment from content providers for prominence and position, and from a cut of the profits on every purchase made through its shopping channel, but its officials admit that it was clearly insufficient then to finance the business, and remains so.

Its parent, Microsoft, had invested vast sums of money in the company around the world, and wanted it to cover costs but in the words of one London official at MSN.co.uk, 'There is always the reach versus revenue balance. And the reach part of it is the most important thing.' [3]

In the case of Amazon.com 'reach' comes from its frontier cowboy image (which it worked hard to acquire and then exploit) and the 70 per cent of its customers who, once having made a purchase, come back for more. As the number of newcomers using the portal for the first time grows, as long as returnee percentage stays the same, its reach expands.

MSN has another tool. Hotmail.

Hotmail is the world's biggest internet operation, with more than 60 million global users in 2000. It was bought by Microsoft and turned into an integral part of MSN. And although as an online e-mailer it is more useful in those countries where telephone calls are unmetered, it still performs the essential function of dragging people back to the MSN site day after day, and sometimes several times a day.

Hotmail has become integral to the lives of millions of users around the world: and every time they click into e-mail they provide a buying opportunity to those shopkeepers on the MSN portal, or for the content providers who contribute to its service.

Hotmail is effectively a community of users, every bit as much as the community that gathers around MSN sports sites, or its family sites, its message boards and chat rooms: or in the real world those who gather at football stadia, weddings, or in local bars to talk.

Communities communicate.

Amazon.com single mindedly, from the beginning, built a database and knowledge of its customers, and it uses that knowledge to keep customers coming back. For example, the database records that on two visits to the site a customer bought a book on Custer's Last Stand and another on the US cavalry. So the software will send him e-mail, and suggest he might like to look at a book on the Seventh Cavalry that they have in stock. If he goes back and buys the book, the software records that, too. The records are updated and Amazon has a clearer idea of where the interests of that consumer lie. It can also garner some idea of his or her income – judged by the price and quantity of books bought – and even if he or she is part of some local community of people with similar interests (all members of a US military history club, for example).

> "hotmail is effectively a community of users"

It continually builds on that knowledge, expanding it and utilizing it – so outstripping rivals such as MSN, which at the start of the new century did not have that capacity.

That has left MSN and every other portal playing catch up, providing tools such as comparison engines, online wallets and searching for a way to provide 'the best experience' that Amazon is ever improving.

When its competitors started to close the gap, Amazon introduced a new feature called 'Where's my stuff?' allowing customers to follow their orders in transit. It worked on the belief that information is a powerful took, and a customer who feels in charge is a satisfied one.

It was right.

of spiders and poderators

Back in 1994, when Yahoo! was also a name for techies, a professor at Carnegie Mellon University in Pittsburgh thought it would be a good idea to have a computer program to go out and catalogue the few hundred websites that had sprung up by that time, providing a service for the handful of internet users who existed and saving them the bother of making up their little notebooks of site locations.

The idea of a program crawling around searching out these sites was a little like the spider Lycosidae, and so Lycos was born.

Nowadays Lycos has been bought by Spain's Terra Networks and is Terra Lycos, but way back at the turn of the century it was still far bigger than many people knew, claiming indeed to provide the widest cover of any portal in Europe.

In Britain its community builder was tripod.co.uk, and the Tripod entity across the whole of Europe had around 800,000 members.[4]

Lycos, it said, was about finding information – basically a search engine true to its origins – and Tripod was 'about expressing yourself and interacting with other people'.

Its mini-communities are called 'pods' and the people who run its chat rooms and message boards, the central focus of the community, are called 'poderators.' It is essentially a community for students, and each community has 'pods' peculiar to its region.

Its UK operation, run by some 50 students from leading universities who classify as 'upstanding members of the community', has a pod called 'Clubbing' – unique because even in the English-speaking world 'clubbing' is a term used mostly in Britain (going out to what used to be called discos). Clubbing is a British phenomenon, and it has become Tripod.co.uk's most popular pod, underscoring the changing demographics of its user base.

Three years ago the most popular pods were computer games, or web technology: now it is clubbing, with music a close second – which suggest the community is growing across a 17–25 year old age group, and with a wider demographic base.

The idea behind Tripod goes against much popular thinking that a single strong brand, a super brand, can appeal to everyone and attract all demographics.

Tripod believes that a super brand will attract a large part of the population but to deliver targeting it is vital to have an extensive reach of all demographics, in essence a portfolio of brands – or pods – that appeal to different communities. And within those communities there will be individuals – catered for in this case by a one-minute homepage builder which allows each community member to create his or her website and publish whatever he or she desires.

Tripod is the community centre of the village, and each pod, each type of different interest user, uses the facilities of rooms within it, free of any charge. It is a fundamentally different way of empowering every member of a community as an individual, but keeping them within the community embrace.

Building a community, Tripod style, is done partly by research, partly by communication, and partly by provision of other services.

Each year up to its merger Lycos had sent out questionnaires online (inviting people to fill them out and have their names put into a prize draw, rather than go through a registration process) asking details on demographics, lifestyle and attitudes.

In 1999 on its contents question it asked people if they wanted maps.

It was an afterthought – but 52 per cent of the people sampled responded that they wanted maps. Lycos responded with a section for maps – providing them kept its members coming back, satisfied members of the community.

Tripod builds the community and facilitates its members' efforts to distinguish themselves within it – but Lycos is also a clear example of the Bezos advice to be a facilitator, and be a networker.

Around the world at the start of the century more than 32 million had signed up for Lycos network services of one kind or another. And within that network it encouraged users to leap from one Lycos network site to another, recirculating the traffic and using its comprehensive range of services.

The whole of the network was worth more than the sum of the parts. Although in Lycos' case the fly is free at any time to leave the spider's web of networks, why would it?

The desired end result is to create a site that has many buying or interest features to it.

The objective is to create a community that returns regularly and has a sense of belonging that reaches tribal levels. The critical issue here is to capture customer data and use them to increase sales.

“the objective is to create a community that returns regularly and has a sense of belonging that reaches tribal levels”

It is to put a tattoo on the chest, and back it with data on the guy who bought the machine, so that the marketing department can call him up and sell him a pair of inscribed Harley boots, a ticket to the next Harley show, or just pat him on the back and say, ‘Thanks for being part of our community.’

Keep them happy. Keep them buying. Keep them.

on parade with the ants

The classic community is the ant colony. It has a queen, it has workers, and it has soldiers – but all actually contribute to the whole. If the object of a community is the welfare of the entire community, then as in the Lycos philosophy, in the ant colony the whole is greater than the sum of the parts.

A community brings elements – ants or people – together. They contribute to it, and it enables them to contribute. And in e-business what a customer portal must do is create the ultimate community by giving people benefits for their contribution, and at the same time make it easy for them to add to their contribution.

The classic example is that of eBay.

CASE STUDY

EBay is to auctions what Robert Stephenson was to the railroad industry – the pioneer that set the world in mass motion. It is not only the world's biggest online auction site, but one of its offshoots in Germany was already the world's third biggest online auction house in its own right at the start of 2000.

It is a consumer-to-consumer affair, by and large, and a prime example of the principle of building an online marketplace. It is equally a superb example of a community at work.

Right from the beginning it took the attitude that its best supporters were the people who used its facilities, who knew how to use its facilities and who would help out those who wanted to use its facilities. So one of its first site considerations was a message board where novices or others could go for advice, and where the experts – the community – could answer them.

Anyone with a question goes to its chat board and asks for information on what it wants to know: the answers come by the stream from other users, and eBay regards the community itself as more powerful than what the company actually does. [5]

It knew it could provide the ordinary FAQ (frequently asked questions) column that most sites offer, but it also understood that a community of eight million users knew more of the answers, and more of the questions too.

Questions like when to trade and when not to trade, when to dig, when not to dig, and is this seller reliable?

EBay has gone through many accusations that auctions on its site are rigged, or that items are not authentic and it has pulled many items from its lists because it had reason to doubt them. It has also banned from its sites those it believed might be rigging auctions.

Of themselves the rigged auctions, the dubious sales, the horror stories (kidneys for sale and so on) are the stuff that business disaster is made of.

But eBay has developed such a strong brand that the curiosity value of such headlines actually acts as a driver to its regional operations – and once registered people become part of its community, and return regularly, if not to buy then to check what they might want to buy.

And when they buy they often take the opportunity to add comments on the reliability, authenticity, and general attitude of the person from whom they buy, to eBay's ratings system.

Feedback in this case is an essential part of the eBay community-building ethos, which it has developed to the stage where today buyers feel compelled to trade on its site because it is so enormous and sellers flock back with regularity because they know it has the most buyers.

content and community lead to commerce

In the e-business world it seems to be interchangeable whether content or community is the beginning. In some cases, such as that of The Ecademy, clearly the community developed around the original content – the 12 e-principles first; but in the case of eBay the content began to grow the community and its content of 3.5 million new auctions, and 400,000 new items posted every day continues to give it its unique community, and business base.

But it is the community that makes eBay what it is.

In both of the alternative approaches – content or community first – the contributions of the community drive growth, and the facilities the company provides to make the contributions easy to deliver and be received drives the community. The end result is still commerce.

Remember Macy's motto: 'Be everywhere, do everything – and never fail to astonish the customer.' It means looking at things from the consumer's view, the community's view.

It means remembering that although a company may offer express delivery, it should not be seen by the consumer as the Pony Express. The expectation that sends a shopper to the online mall can easily turn into the frustration that sends him next time to the off-line one.

> “although a company may offer express delivery, it should not be seen by the consumer as the Pony Express”

(According to a survey by the Boston Consulting Group in June 2000, 19 per cent of online e-tail customers said delivery of their orders took longer than they expected, or never occurred at all. Many stopped shopping online, others refused to do any further business with the offending retailer.)

The key in the e-tailing sector is to offer more than point-and-click ordering convenience to build the brand and keep the customers loyal:

it is providing a full shopping experience, mouse to house.

This is why same-day service is already becoming a fixture in the USA. Barnesandnoble.com guarantee delivery in Manhattan by 7 pm for internet orders placed by 11 am; in Los Angeles, toys or other items ordered from Sameday.com by 2 pm will arrive at the home by 8 pm.

> “the key in the e-tailing sector is to offer a full shopping experience, mouse to house”

Companies like Amazon.com, as mentioned earlier also provide customers with the means to track the status of any shipment. It is a service to their community.

Communities come in many shapes, and attached to many sectors, from the auction houses to the portal clubs, from the online shopping malls through to the special interest groups. In The Ecademy's view they all come together under the 11th principle, one which after all the infrastructure is in place and all the support built in, is key to creating a lasting brand which keeps its customers coming back for more.

The idea of community as a commercial tool is not new: the merchants guilds of mediaeval times, the co-operative societies of the late 19th century, the friendly societies and building societies in their early days – all examples of the community building principle at work.

What the internet adds is global reach, and the opportunity for 24-hour-a-day interaction. What the e-business gets back is increased use, increased information, increased sales.

Power is in people.

notes

1 Interestingly, George Heilmeier of Texas Instruments also managed to get himself in the quote books by saying that every time his company had an opportunity to 'run our R & D scientists and engineers against our customers, we do it'.

2 See Battle of the Portals, Thomas Power and George Jerjian, Ecademy 1999.

3 Interview with Geoff Sutton, MSN, December 10, 1999.

4 Interview with Charles Walker, Lycos, December 21, 1999.

5 Interview with Alexis de Belloy, EBay, January 24, 2000.

14 the only claim to importance: personalization

"In mountain warfare in general we should observe that everything depends... on the morale of our soldiers. Here it is not a question of skilful manoeuvering, but of warlike spirit and wholehearted devotion to the cause, for each man is left to act more or less individually"

Principles of War Defensive 7

What if someone sent you an e-mail which showed that they knew all sorts of things about you, your wants, and your purchasing habits. Would you be thrilled – or would you run screaming from Big Brother?

There is some very good predictive software out on the marketplace today. But implementation is almost always scaled back because the software can seem too invasive. Here is the opportunity: if you can integrate the predictive power of such software and combine it with a vibrant community where there is lots of external communication, you will have an insight into the marketplace that will massively outstrip your competition's. You will also create an enormous barrier to entry in the marketplace. Think about this

How many clubs do you want to join? If there isn't some real benefit then you are just annoyed by the intrusion of yet more junk mail and information. If you are the club controlling the conversation which surrounds your marketplace, then your access to information is primary. And the more of it you are willing to share back, the less likely someone else will be to break into your community ownership.

TWELFTH PRINCIPLE

Personalization is the way you reintegrate into the community of all the assets and information you collect. The tools are simple, but beware of trying to control too much. If you send a cookie to every member's computer and record their every keystroke on and off-line, you would expect an angry response. You have to treat the community as an asset, rather than a possession.

summary

- beware of seeming to know too much about your customers
- if you can create the right atmosphere, you will be able to use your information in more subtle and useful ways
- share information
- a community is an asset, not a possession

EVEN IN AN IMPERSONAL, technological age, at the end of a business transaction is mostly a person.

That reality reinforces one of the oldest adages in business practices, other than for Henry Ford who could afford to foist black on everybody because of the demand for his product – People Matter.[1]

Although the web is the technology of today, and the future, paradoxically it also demands return to a very old-fashioned value: personalized contact with customers (personalization).

“even in an impersonal, technological age, at the end of a business transaction is mostly a person”

It does not come over the counter, on the shop floor or through a physical knock at the door, but contact with a customer has been at the heart of success for companies such as Amazon.com, and the centre of chaos for others who have chosen to ignore it.

The tragedy is that there has never before been a tool such as the internet which allows a company to know with any exactitude what the individual customer really wants, or is likely to buy: and never has there been an easier, cheaper way to reach the customer with the offer.

The internet is the market analyst, the tele-salesman, and the postman rolled into one.

It can monitor and analyze the buying habits of visitors to a site, customize products and information to match those habits, and respond to queries and requests.

Properly structured and organized, and backed with the right understanding of what a consumer really needs, internet sites can build and enhance relationships through 'personalization'.

In the old days marketing strategy was based on the one-to-one approach, which means seller sells to buyer. The internet has reversed this relationship and created the one-from-one relationship, which means buyer buys from seller. It follows that the better the sellers understand the buyers, the better they can serve them and retain their custom.

The key to that is making a company, a service, as personal as possible to the customer who is using it.

But the awesome power of personalization for the seller is in its ability to create loyalty.

Technology which allows an e-commerce company to create dedicated pages for a specific customer builds an environment where the customer comes back time and time again and the experience becomes unique to that individual.

> “the internet is the market analyst, the tele-salesman, and the postman rolled into one”

Once a customer has spent time personalizing the service at a particular site; he or she is less likely to switch to a competitor. This is a relationship that exists across national boundaries, across time zones and around the clock, and in the business-to-business sector it still allows an e-company to provide a custom offering, with specialized attention to its top accounts, cementing relationships, and maximizing the benefit of an electronic operation.

This is where even the lowly but ubiquitous e-mail becomes a tool of unimagined strength. Coupled with so-called push technology, and software which provides filtering, targeted marketing services, purchase identification, internet relationship management, and matchmaking capability it provides a tool the like of which marketing directors have never seen, and a salesman that sales directors might die for.

a new way to fly

In this world, where the individual matters, there are many ways of making certain that at all times each employee, each executive, and each customer is provided with the personal information that is wanted. In a major company environment this goes beyond the aspect of providing information and personal services to the consumer – it strikes right into the heart of a business need to make certain that the right information gets to every staff member.

Not just mission-critical information, but the wider information that plays a part in making the employee better informed, feeling more a part of the company, and which helps him or her place their work in the wider context.

In 1999 British Aerospace, the fourth largest defence company in the world, knew it needed a different system to communicate with its 48,000 employees. It had the internet and intranet, designed to facilitate the retrieval of information, but the systems it had in place were entirely reliant upon keyword searches and manual indexing – an arbitrary, unreliable, impersonal and costly way of unearthing information.

What it needed was a true space age way of keeping its staff up to date and informed.

It wanted to be able automatically to organize information from over 300 internet sites – its own, many heavyweight databases and 12,000 to 15,000 live news feeds – and personalize that information for each user, automatically, without costly manual intervention.

It saw this built into a system that would also eliminate duplication of employee effort by alerting them to existing relevant information, and proactively deliver information to users as they went about their everyday business, dispensing with the need for searches.

It also had concept ideas – building teams through virtual communities, automatically putting users with related or mutual interests in contact with each other, and the greatest buzz phrase of all, 'Utilizing the company's greatest asset – its people'.

CASE STUDY

Enter Autonomy, a British company that approaches the problem of information retrieval through artificial intelligence and which has risen to the top of the UK technological pile with its ideas. Its commercial solution is technology that categorizes, tags, and hyperlinks large volumes of information. Gone are labour-intensive information retrieval chores, gone the need for hordes of human researchers, poring over the internet news feeds or paging through books and magazines.

On the way, the technology generates real-time user profiles, based on the pages users visit and the documents they publish. It uses that information to personalize the information delivered, from breaking news, through to relevant documents elsewhere on the intranet, or the contact details of other people in the company whose interests and expertise match those of the user.

(For those of a technical bent the technology is powered by a pattern-matching technology, which is based upon two fundamental principles – Bayesian Inference and Shannon's Information Theory. This pattern-matching technology actually identifies, understands, and extracts the ideas expressed within digital documents, and is able to locate documents containing similar information. It understands information that is completely unstructured. There is no need for it to be tagged or ordered into fields.)

When it was introduced to British Aerospace systems, from the point of view of staff it meant that not only were they suddenly getting personal information geared to their own preferences and search patterns, but they were getting all the information relevant to their jobs or team operations without having to waste time looking.

What it meant to BAe was pure bottom line. Companies of its size can waste up to £2,500 per day on staff spending time in often fruitless searches for information. But through the technology every member of staff now has instant access to relevant information and business intelligence, delivered in fully personalized style. Documents once circulated in disparate forms – hard copy, HTML, e-mail text, word processing files etc. – are now grouped into directories based on an automatic understanding of their content, concentrating similar resources in the same repository.

Employees get alerts on information they can use and are automatically linked into appropriate interest communities. And its virtual university,

an intranet-based training initiative, can even create a personalized development syllabus for each employee, based on automatic profiling of his or her current expertise and areas of interest.
Ian Black, Head of Corporate Communications and Public Affairs at BAe called it, 'capturing and sharing our organization's hidden intellectual capital'.
Others just call it good business.
At the heart of Autonomy's software is the ability to analyze a document, extract the ideas from the text and determine which are the most important. It does it by using proprietary pattern-matching technology developed by researchers from Cambridge University.
Because Autonomy's technology can derive meaning in a piece of text, it can also profile users by analyzing the ideas in the documents they read or produce. The original product has been modified to suit the use of a range of businesses, from corporate information portals, to online publishing companies and retailers, general business and even for the wireless world.

Up to the last years of the past century knowledge management within most organizations was focussed on putting large structured data warehouses together and then having power tools that would allow trained staff to get the information out. The assumption was that the staff knew the questions that had to be asked.

But the reality of the internet world is that it has dumped billions of pages of unstructured information in a company's lap. In a typical organization, the ratio of unstructured to structured is about 10 to 1, with unstructured information doubling every 12 months, according to META Group.

Add to that a basic flaw in traditional reasoning – that no one knows all the right questions for the answers sought and under old search methods, geared to key word searches that is a prerequisite – the man hours involved could be staggering.

Staff had to pose a question, look at what came back and if it was insufficient, inappropriate or just wrong – as frequently happened – rephrase the question and start again.

Artificial intelligence à la Autonomy returns a result that causes the searcher to navigate down a particular path. In personalization terms it starts from the proposition that no one likes surfing on the internet. What people actually like to do is get to useful information quickly.

In the case of a vacationer, looking for a hang-gliding week in Turkey, he or she goes online to be presented with suggestions of six holidays that are similar, not to go from site to site learning about the scenic attractions of Turkey, or the ideal weather conditions for hang-gliding – he wants the two put together in one package and then tied in with what package tour operators have to offer.

That is where personalization built into the system is the value.

Personalization is all about interacting with the content. Autonomy gains an understanding of what interests the user and then uses that to target him.

It uses spiders to crawl the world, according to parameters, avoiding anything with referred words and automatically bringing back what conforms to the specifications into the engine. With development the company believes it will create a personalized intelligent information service that delivers exactly the right information a user wants, exactly when he needs it – no matter where it happens to be: on the web, on the hard drive, in electronic mail.

“personalization is all about interacting with the content”

Autonomy developed its engine with business in mind – so successfully that it has become one of the world's leading suppliers of artificial intelligence to some of the biggest commercial industrial multinationals.

But early in 2000 it showed its commercial savvy by producing a consumer cut-down version, Kenjin, which can sit on a desktop and do some of its big brother's jobs in a way that may appeal to an ordinary consumer at home.

With sound business sense, and a clearly displayed knowledge of the things that internet users want, Autonomy made that free.

getting to know all about you

In late 1999 MSN.co.uk, the local branch of Microsoft Network in Britain, believed it ranked second or third in the most visited ratings, vying for top spot in real terms with Yahoo! and Freeserve, the ISP started by the British electrical retail chain Dixon's.

Reports by the various measurement firms seemed to confirm this.

In a large part Freeserve's place at the top, and MSN's was down to a particular fact: both were the default pages installed on many computers when bought. In the case of Freeserve it was installed on every computer sold by its then parent, Dixon's, through its high street stores and its PC World and Curry's outlets. In the case of MSN it was picked out as the homepage by Internet Explorer, which by that time had become the de facto browser standard, despite the hard core of millions still using Netscape or other browsers on other hardware platforms as well as the Wintel combination.

MSN was then recording about 5.8 million 'unique' visitors a month; that is, people who went once or more, but not counting anything after the first visit.

But it had no idea of their profile. Many were funnelled directly from the Microsoft's homepage and all the traffic monitors did was tell MSN.co.uk in London that there had been a hit.

It had a rough idea that the bulk of the traffic was male, and that it slotted into the ABC1 bracket but there was nothing scientific about that assumption. It was based on general demographics – which at that stage still showed more males than females online, although it has since changed – on the acceptance that since much of its traffic came from the Internet Explorer default it was probable those visiting followed the average makeup of the surfing population.

But until the commercial research reports by outside organizations began to show that women internet users were on the increase – in early 1999 – it had done nothing to provide content which might appeal to women, or to design the site in a way that would hold more attraction for the female browser.

It did not even track the visitors to its site in depth. It tracked clicks, and knew what was popular and what was doing well but it did not know who the user was, and only up to a point could it work out what pattern of activity an individual user had.[2]

Neither did it have a database of users who visited the site. In the words of one of its senior British officials: 'We were quite a long way off being where we would have liked to be in order to build a relationship with our customers.'

That admission typifies the attitude of even major players in the e-business world, who have yet to understand what their own technology can do for them.

In the case of MSN it could not profile its users: no profiling meant no personalization and no capacity to add value by trying to capture them as loyal users of the site.

“profiling systems are at the heart of the personalization process”

Profiling systems are at the heart of the personalization process: some are insidious and incur the wrath of privacy groups (by the middle of 2000 those were heading towards the sin bin) but carefully used, in a transparent fashion they are the very essence of the way Amazon.com has managed to tailor its product.

Order a book from Amazon.com and it goes into your personal profile: by carefully watching each time a book is ordered, the Amazon technology develops an understanding of what your preferences are, and very soon is able to send out e-mails suggesting what it has new on its cyber shelves which might be of interest.

Early in 2000 it began test marketing an addition. It adapted its software so that the technology was able to feed into an individual user homepage a message, not just about new books but about older ones which might be laying on its cyber shelves, and which came within the preference range it had determined.

"it was just another step down the personal homepage road"

It was just another step down the personal homepage road.

It was following the principle of the last chapter: customer involvement builds the community.

But personalization cements the relationship and keeps the customer coming back, and spreading by word of mouth to others that this is a good and caring community to be in.

the website is flat

Content is the product in any store.

It is the clothes on the shelves, the candy in serve-it-yourself plastic trays, and the bottles in the refrigerated cabinet.

What an astute business needs to do, and what the old street corner storekeeper used to do by instinct or by his knowledge of his customers, is marry that content to the individual. He would not suggest liquor to the Methodist minister who had just come through the door, or comment on a new bikini for a woman he knew was a confirmed naturist. He would carefully keep the candy away from the couple on a diet.

But to do that he also had to understand the content – the candy could be sugar free, the liquor without alcohol. Even the bikini could be the kind that dissolves in water.

Many companies know their websites are flat. They have the content but they don't really understand it or really how to use it. It is not presented in a way that encourages the visitor to explore it, and there is no appreciation of how to exploit it so that the customer knows what it is, because they do not know the customer anyway.

On the best pages on media sites the news is tagged under headings that enable a vistor to click on a line and go straight to the section that corresponds to his interest. Where the element of personalization comes in is the way the technology tracks that content: it can pick up how many times a woman visits a boxing site, or even a boxing story, and ignores one on cricket. In time it knows that she likes boxing and dislikes cricket, so the next time Mike Tyson is in town it can post a little message on her homepage, or send her an e-mail asking if she would like to order a ticket.

Some companies take the attitude that by making the supply of detailed information a prerequisite for entry to the site, this will itself provide the detail that is needed to achieve a more personal service.

> “many companies know their websites are flat”

But in the atomic world, when two people meet for the first time, rarely do they immediately begin to exchange their personal secrets. That has to wait until they know each other much better. This applies equally in the internet world: when a person clicks onto a company site and is greeted with a long questionnaire, the reaction may well be, ‘Why the hell should I tell these guys everything about me’, and click away.

Profiling takes the softly softly approach: track the visitor quietly in the background, find out about him as he clicks through the site. Some people object but compare that to walking and shopping in a supermarket: the eyes of the security cameras are everywhere, and no one objects. So too with profiling technology. It all happens without the site operator having to ask any questions, or be visible.

In time a site can even reconstruct itself to suit the way an individual it has been tracking, moves around. And that will mean in time that every site will be different for every person.

Monitoring, matching, and, ultimately, marrying. The relationship rules.[3]

the art of survival

In the end it is about success. But before that it is about survival, and personalization is one of the tools a company can use to survive.

Survival is more than a dictionary definition of avoiding termination.

In the business world it is making sure a company is ready to handle a rapid increase in the scale of those who are going to be visiting, it is about knowing the demographic groups that will visit and about looking into the future and defining a way to adapt to new technologies which are so far only a spot of light at the end of a pipeline.

In each of these three aspects the lynchpin to support competitiveness and survival is once again personalization.[4]

That means adapting the experience that a business gives to someone online, according to any different number of attributes or preferences that person may have. It may be the type of customer he is, or as simple as the language he prefers to use.

In the technology world there already are existing solutions that can detect that the browser on the site is French, simply through the settings that are picked up. So the personalization package begins with a short message asking if the browser would like to see the version in French.

There is instant communication: no need to click on a button, the technology does it first.

The technology can tell if the access is being made from a WAP (wireless application protocol) phone – the lesson follows that the user does not want heavy streamed content. So if the WAP phone is calling from France the technology enables a company to deliver curt information in French. This, in the words of Matt Price of Art Technology Group, is the five seconds and two clicks that a company has to differentiate itself from its competitors. The competitive arrival for survival.

Even in 1999 Letsbuyit.com, the collective buying company founded in Sweden, registered in Holland and based in England, was asking anyone browsing its site which country they came from and giving them one click to get them through to the content in their own language, with their own language and local pricing.

That is the first element, the most basic element of personalization without any form of profiling.

The message to sceptical traditional CEOs is put something up, then listen and be sensitive. Technology is just a small part of it. The approach is more important.

On any website the company is the fine-feathered swan sitting on top of the water, preening its feathers while it coasts along. The technology is the legs and feet thrashing around unseen under the water, driving it serenely along – unseen by all the people feeding it cakes and tidbits.

No one sees it, few worry about it, but it is the means that a company has to ensure its survival: it is the thrashing legs and the webbed feet that prevent the corporate swan being washed away downstream by the current of the river.

And when the time comes and the feeding is done, and the hunter comes along with a gun, it is the technology that enables the corporate swan to flap its wings, thrash its feet, lift up to skim along the surface and then up into the air.

The wise CEO will admit that he does not know what is going to happen next year and will put in the technology, the infrastructure, to manage what may eventuate anyway.

That may be a contradiction but it's the only way to fly.

notes

1 Even Ford said that while 'all Fords are alike, no two men are just alike'. It was part of his advice to young men where he told them: 'Every new life is a new thing under the sun: there has never been anything like it before, never will be again. A young man ought to get that idea about himself, he should look for the single spark of individuality that makes him different from the other folks, and develop that for all he is worth. Society and schools may try to iron it out of him: their tendency is to put it all in the same mold, but I say don't let that spark be lost. It is your only real claim to importance.'

2 Interview with Geoff Sutton, MSN.co.uk, December 10, 1999.

3 Interview with Rebekah Menenez, Vignette, January 20, 2000.

4 Interview with Matt Price, Art Technology Group, January 4, 2000.

15 conclusion

"The great difficulty is this. TO REMAIN FAITHFUL THROUGHOUT TO THE PRINCIPLES WE HAVE LAID DOWN FOR OURSELVES. ... No battle has convinced me as much as this one [the Battle of Menin, 1794] that we must not despair of success until the last moment. It proves that the influence of good principles, which never manifests itself as often as we expect, can suddenly reappear ... when we have already given up hope of their influence"

Principles of War

Principles in Time of War

WHEN LARRY ELLISON, CEO of Oracle Corporation, said, 'The internet changes everything', some analysts believed it was another case of internet executive hyperbole. In hindsight, it was an understatement.[1] The internet has changed and will continue to change every aspect of our lives and our businesses on a continuous and unrelenting basis. Perhaps almost all of us have a problem with that, because although most are prepared to change, few are reluctant to change so swiftly. When things change too swiftly, people worry they too will quickly become obsolete.

> "when things change too swiftly, people worry they too will quickly become obsolete"

The answer, for the businessman, is that like the rest of the world he needs to be in a constant state of learning simply to stay afloat. But to excel at what he does, he will need to do more than just learn. He will need to be flexible. He will need to be adaptable. He will need to learn to enjoy 'learning'. If he does not, his existence will be marginally better than miserable.

A consumer is more than just a customer who buys, or uses products, services and information, produced by an organization. A consumer is also a producer or worker inside or outside an organization, to which he contributes his skills in return for pay.

This consumer also needs to learn because, although in this new economy, he is left with little time and much stress and unless he is prepared to start once again absorbing information about this new age and his place in it, he may find himself redundant in a short period of time. Things will not get better for the consumer/employee.

His only real option is the same as that facing the company which employs him – to be flexible, to be adaptable, and to want to learn.

In this same world the consumer as user is increasing in value to businesses.

That in turn means businesses have to pay him more attention than ever before. They have little choice, neither should they need encouragement, to use the tools the internet has placed in their hands to pay him the attention he needs, and exploit the loyalty that brings.

The technology is there for businesses to use through the internet to follow a customer's behaviour, to track his purchases, finances, and lifestyles, monitor his dietary choices and health, learn what he wears in styles of clothing, how he spends his increasing leisure and where he goes and what he prefers in his travel pursuits.

This is not, of necessity, the Big Brother insidious environment some commentators picture.

Continuous feedback allows businesses to anticipate and service customers' needs on a constant open-ended basis. Since when, the question arises, is service considered an evil?

> “since when is service considered an evil?”

Jeremy Rifkin is a fellow at Wharton School Executive Education Programme and author of *The Age of Access: The New Culture of Hypercapitalism where all Life is a Paid-for Experience.*

In his book[2] he says that:

> In the old industrial economy, each person's labor power was considered a form of property that could be sold in the marketplace. In the new networked economy, selling access to one's day-to-day living patterns and

life experiences, as reflected in purchasing decisions, becomes a much sought-after intangible asset.

The transformation in the nature of commerce from selling items to commodifying relationships and creating communities marks a turning point in the way commerce is conducted.

To belong is to be connected to the many networks that make up the new global economy. Being a subscriber, member or client becomes as important as being propertied. It is, in other words, access rather than ownership that increasingly determines one's status in the coming age.

But the message to businesses is not just about the advantages they can reap. It is equally about the dangers that they face. Many have already seen the light.

They have seen the savings to be gained by moving their procurement to the electronic network. They are continuing to do so. But not all can survive, and the consolidation that was already underway at the time this book was being written will already have seen many casualties by the time it is published.

“the 21st century's way of doing trade and commerce, by clicks and mortar operations”

We are entering a time when the media, the analysts, the consultants, and the public will stop talking about e-business or e-commerce, or about the cyber sector, and the bricks and mortar. We are entering the age when Big Business and dot coms will merge into new entities built on a combination of both worlds. The 21st century's way of doing trade and commerce, by clicks and mortar operations.

That is a transformation already well underway.

The next revolution which it will spark is still approaching: the time when even these businesses find they can no longer retain the attention of their customers and the cost of attempting to do so is becoming prohibitively expensive.

This is the age of the new war: the coming war between the portals, more aggressive, more fierce than the battle for online supremacy that marked the end of the last century.

In his book, *The Practice of Management*, published in 1954, Peter Drucker, the grand old man of management science, wrote: 'Because its purpose is to create a customer, the business enterprise has only two basic functions: marketing and innovation. Marketing and innovation produce results. All the rest are costs'.[3]

As the marketing perspective overtakes the production perspective, organizing consumption overtakes organizing production and becomes the order of the day. The key is to find the appropriate mechanism to hold onto the customer for life.

“the key is to find the appropriate mechanism to hold onto the customer for life”

Which is where more than 40 years later Drucker returned in an article entitled, 'Can e-commerce deliver?' to make three insightful comments:

> In most businesses today, delivery is considered a 'support' function. Under e-commerce, delivery will become the one area in which a business can truly distinguish itself. It will become the critical 'core competence'.
>
> For the first time in business history, e-commerce separates selling and purchasing. Selling is completed when the order has been received and paid for. Purchasing is completed only when the purchase has been delivered and actually not until it satisfies the purchaser's want.
>
> In traditional business structures, selling is still seen and organized as a servant to production or as a cost center that sells what we make.
>
> In the future, e-commerce companies will sell what we can deliver.[4]

In the coming war the businesses that succeed will be those that can carry with them the traditional lessons of business, hone them with the new tools available to them, and then meld them with the new paradox that the anonymity of the internet is creating a world where people need to be treated increasingly as individuals, but equally as part of a loyal community.

It is as a guide to the ways to prepare for this war that The Ecademy's '12 Principles' were developed.

“the anonymity of the internet is creating a world where people need to be treated increasingly as individuals, but equally as part of a loyal community”

Some call them guidelines, some call them an 'ecosystem', and some call them a process, or a set of principles or rules.

Von Clausewitz says in his great work, *On War*, the measured academic work on which he worked until he died in 1827, and which built on the hastily written *Principles*, that the purpose of any theory is to clarify concepts and ideas that have become confused and entangled. He suggests that not until the terms and concepts have been defined can one hope to make any progress in examining the question clearly. He added, in a comment that might have been written with the economic war that is now beginning in mind, that 'a theory need not be a positive doctrine, a sort of manual for action'. He went on to write:

> Whenever an activity deals primarily with the same things again and again, with the same ends and the same means, these things are susceptible of rational study.
>
> It is precisely that inquiry which is the most essential part of any theory... it is an analytical investigation leading to a close acquaintance with the subject applied to experience [in our case to e-commerce] and leads to a thorough familiarity with it.
>
> The closer it gets to that goal, the more it proceeds from the objective form of a science to the subjective form of a skill, the more effective it will prove in areas where the nature of the case admits no arbiter but talent.

Call it theory, call it principle, von Clausewitz believed that such ideas need to be put down in easily understandable form so that someone coming into the arena need not start afresh each time sorting out the material and ploughing through it:

It is meant to educate the mind of the future commander, or more accurately to guide him in his self education, not to accompany him to the battlefield – just as a wise teacher guides and stimulates a young man's intellectual development, but is careful not to lead him by the hand for the rest of his life.

[And his] principles and rules are intended to provide a thinking man with a frame of reference for the movements he has been trained to carry out, rather than to serve as a guide which at the moment of action lays down precisely the path he must take.[5]

“make no mistake: the war is coming”

This book is not intended as a scaffolding holding up a completed piece of architecture: like Gaudi's cathedral masterpiece in Barcelona, e-business is in the process of development, and all there can be are guides which point down paths on which the builder can safely travel.

But the ‘Principles’ are a thinking businessman's frame of reference for the future, meant to educate the mind of the commanders in the future war.

For make no mistake: the war is coming. It is every commander's duty to be ready for it.

notes

1 Oracle Corporation 1999 annual report.

2 The Age of Access: The New Culture of Hypercapitalism where all Life is a Paid-for Experience, Jeremy Rifkin, Industry Standard, March 20, 2000.

3 The Hutchinson Dictionary of Business Quotations, Helicon Publishing, Oxford, 1996, page 34.

4 'The World in 2000', an Economist publication, Business and Management section, page 122.

5 On War, Carl von Clausewitz, pages 133–141.

small tales

the hat man

There are only about 350 people living in Congerville, Illinois. Small towns don't get much smaller. It has no grocery store, no service station, just a grain silo, a few houses and a tiny post office.

And an outpost of global commerce.

Congerville is the home of Noggintops.com, a global supplier of high quality men's hats.

Hatmaker Doug Young says he chose Congerville because he likes living in the country. One would have to. It doesn't get more country than this.

And he likes having an online store because it lets his family live where they like without worrying about locations.

His business started because he is an avid outdoorsman and had trouble finding high quality stylish hats to fit his lifestyle, even elsewhere on the internet.

He used to stop at country stores when he was out, checking out the hats and finding them wanting.

Then in September 1999 he and his wife decided to do it themselves.

They researched the subject (Principle 1), planned the operations through contact with consultants they found off the web (Principle 2), then checked out the suppliers' situation and how to best get the small quantities they needed at the right price (Principle 9).

The need for hardware and software (Principle 3) was hardly huge and there was no network (Principle 4) so Young quit his job as a counsellor in Bloomington, Illinois, and opened the business. Some 3,000 people a week were visiting the site in mid-July 2000 and he was selling 100 hats a week, mostly through a credit card payment system (Principle 6).

From the site he sells everything from straw hats to fedoras and the bush hats worn by Canadian soldiers in the Gulf War.

He buys his supplies from makers in the USA, Australia, Ireland, England and Austria (Principle 7).

His marketing is through adverts in five fishing and three hunting magazines and he answers all e-mails himself (Principle 10).

He says he tries to come as close as possible to personalizing customers to give them the kind of treatment they would expect if they were physically in his store, even phoning them by old-fashioned voice means if he has to (Principle 12).

Now he has built up a community of customers who come back for other hats like the ones they have seen in old movies, or in black and white photographs and they send him other customers (Principle 11).

Mr Young says he is doing very well, thank you.

'People who are familiar with shopping on the internet seem very surprised when they get a little extra', he said.

http://www.noggintops.com

the vision

Stratton Sclavos, the Chief Executive of VeriSign, sees a future with a magical number which will 'unify my fragmented digital self'.

He believes that the number will be an IP (internet protocol) address which will replace a phone number and will instead link all phone numbers, e-mail addresses, websites and portable computing devices associated with an individual.

As he moves around the world, his digital identity will go with him, making it easier for anyone to communicate through any method.

Through the routing networks the handling company will know what is lit up on its network at any given time in terms of device or location, and will route traffic there.

He calls it the 'universal location' idea.

And believes that it is 'cool' (*Washington Post*, July 7, 2000).

It is easy to see why VeriSign has this vision, given that in 2000 it bought Network Solutions, the guardian of the master database of internet domain names.

But in fact the vision of NS goes even further. Its Chief Executive, Jim Rutt, says that everyone will have a domain name as a master internet address, and then there will be subdomain names to locate him anywhere and via every device.

He gave the example of www.billclinton.com and www.bedroom.TV.billclinton.com

If you are at the office and want to check on the status of your home air conditioning on a hot day, you could just type in its domain name and see if it is working.

This is what is now being called super-DNS, the next generation internet domain name system that will be tailored for a world in which, as the *Washington Post* said, even vegetables at the grocery store may be monitored by the internet.

Domain names were invented to help people avoid having to type in highly complicated combinations of numbers as they did in the early days of the internet. Super-DNS takes it one step further.

Sclavos believes it will take several years to design an addressing scheme flexible enough to manage the devices which already exist and which will emerge. He also admitted that no one is sure that a system can be designed to handle the enormous scale required.

Something, however, has to be done.

The estimates are that today's domain name system will reach its limit at about 4 billion IP addresses and in mid-2000 it was already halfway there.

http://www.verisign.com

http://www.networksolutions.com

the shatterer of myths

Ray Elsey is the man who shatters myths.

In 2000 he went into his fourth year of online retailing, and his fourth year of profitability – almost unheard of in a dot com world where e-tailers are expected to lose money, survive on their wits, and then go out of business. And he did it without selling books, or CDs or other domestically demanded low-cost items.

Elsey started Tradeshop in 1996 as an online jewellery store in Los Angeles, and he took home $1.1 million in profit on gross revenue of $4.5 million in 1998. In 1999 that revenue had more than doubled.

His secret is elusive. He designed his website himself, and programmed it himself: it is clearly homespun right down to the spelling errors which the *Los Angeles Times* described (April 26, 2000) as 'so pervasive that after noticing the 15th error it ceases to be annoying and becomes entertaining'.

It may be that his markup on his jewellery is only 12 to 25 per cent, against an industry standard of about 300 per cent, it may be the very homespun feel of his site that has given him a repeat customer business that ranges from college students through to Fortune 100 executives spending $7,000 each time they shop.

He has even done engraving for Bill Gates and says he has sold quite a few items in the five-figure range to Microsoft's everyday employees.

One of the things Tradeshop did was to establish credibility – trust – among its customers. It did it by posting all of its banking references, corporate account profiles and bank officer contact information on its site.

It also built a custom creations area, catering at times to those on limited budgets but with big ambitions, like the college graduate who only had $350 to spare for his engagement ring and ended up with a custom-crafted solitaire with a one-third carat diamond – way out of the range of the off-line suppliers he had contacted.

Said Elsey, 'He personifies why I am doing this.'

Elsey also says that the internet has removed the danger from custom work the company does. In the past special requests were handled over the phone: now he uses the internet to send drawings of designs and get comments back so that in the end the buyer knows exactly what he is getting and there is a 100 per cent satisfaction rate.

But one suspects he almost got beaten once.

A customer sent him an e-mail wanting a re-creation of the Ring of Babbahar from J.R.R.Tolkien's *Lord of the Rings*.

'It is the most interesting job I have ever done on the web,' he says. 'We now use it to show folks we can build anything.'

And his online business? 'I have learned that I can dream bigger than I dared imagine. I feel like Willie Wonka in a magic world making magical things in a magical way.'

http://www.tradeshop.com

beam me down, scotty In Valencia, California, 3D Systems makes what the *New York Times* calls a three-dimensional fax machine (June 11, 2000).

Instead of pushing out a piece of paper with a design on it, it produces an actual object, a bit like the replicator in the 'Star Trek' incarnations, but not – as yet – with items edible.

It uses a thermo-jet office printer working from a digital blueprint to squirt out hot plastic and make something in the shape of a blender, or a car, or a carrot. It is a prized tool in the world of industrial design.

What it has to do with the world of e-business is simple: it is accessible to people all over the world, who can now collaborate on projects that would have been impossible just a couple of years ago.

Its importance lies, as the *New York Times* said, in the significance of that remote working: the internet is making possible a truly virtual conglomerate with no headquarters, no shipping, no warehouses, no infrastructure at all and 'a company that is no more than the sum of its ever changing parts'.

The idea is not a new one. In 1992 William Davidow, an ex-Intel Vice-President, co-authored a book called *The Virtual Corporation*, in which he predicted that the flow of electronic information would allow companies to decentralize themselves, and spin off functions such as product development, manufacturing, inventory manages, even sales and returns.

He ignored all the ridicule and criticism that followed and put his money into companies such as Agile Software, and Datasweep that produce software allowing established companies to morph into virtual entities.

Davidow says that so much of what is seen in the internet business-to-business space is 'about having the ability to co-ordinate relationships between different entities'.

The result of all this spinning off is lower cost. The prime example is Cisco Systems, whose internet routers are assembled by an independent manufacturer from parts provided by different suppliers, overseen by another company which tracks the inventory and supplies. Cisco just provides the R&D and the sales force.

As a result of this lower cost the 3D printer fetched $100,000 in 1997 but because of the cost cutting involved in its production this figure reduced to $50,000 by the time of the *New York Times* article and could be as low as $1,000 in the not so distant future.

Massachusetts Institute of Technology is working on a 3D printer that will print in several colours, and in time every home-based designer will be able to afford his own.

The headline on the *Times* story by David Pescovitz summed it up nicely. It called 3D Systems 'the company where everybody is a temp'.

http://www.3dsystems.com

a veritable scream

Since November 1999 Mark Jung at the Minneapolis Institute of Arts has had a hot product on his hands. Inflatable versions of the Edvard Munch painting, The Scream.

He sells them over the web where they are much faster sellers than the items in the Institute's gift shop where only three or four have been sold.

When online customers want to buy the four-feet high Scream they go first to the website, and are then diverted to Museumshop.com, which designed the virtual store and processes its orders.

The alliance is one of the more unusual on the web – museums with contents that span the centuries turning to new age experts in the 21st century marketing field.

Rebecca Reynolds, founder of MuseumShop, says that some museum administrators have realized that a lot goes into the problem of making sure that online customers are interested and happy and will come back again, and appear to prefer to leave it in the hands of professionals, while just raking in the extra profits.

The museums, meanwhile, present entrepreneurs such as her with a vast source of cultural resource and marketable reproductions.

According to the American Association of Museums, gift shops and publications accounted for 7.3 per cent of museum revenue in 1997, the latest date for which information is available.

MuseumNetwork, another of the web entrepreneurs (there is another called MuseumCompany.com) estimates that the global market for museum merchandising is $10 billion a year, of which three-quarters is outside the USA.

MOMA (Museum of Modern Art) – always one of the world's most aggressive galleries – preferred to keep its cash at home. It has developed a sophisticated website to work hand in hand with its equally sophisticated and long established mail-order operations, and instead of partnering with dot com companies, it is forging a link with Britain's Tate.

Nevertheless the web entrepreneurs in mid-2000 believed they had found the pot of gold at the end of the artistic rainbow.

David Bearman, president of Archives and Museum Informatics, which organizes the annual museums and the web conference in Minneapolis, said that all of those in the scene were betting they had the magic formula.

And as might befit a custodian in the antiquarian sector he added sagely, 'Of course, nobody knows what that magic formula is.'

http://www.moma.com

http://www.museumshop.com

http://www.museumnetwork.com

http://www.museumcompany.com

monica's story

Everybody knows Monica Lewinsky's story. Or at least part of it. What some may not know is the sequel.

After the White House affair, she decided to go into the handbag business, drawing on her experience designing costumes for high school plays.

She knitted some and sold some to friends who told her to go sell them in the shops.

She did some research, wrote a 'mission statement' and then went onto the web. Undoubtedly, the global recognition of the name worked wonders, because between October 1999 and July 2000, Monica's site had more than 5,000,000 hits.

She sold the first handbag at Bendel's in March 2000 and she started to get 'tons' of e-mail, for which she hired a handling service.

She designs the bags, while four partners with a background in business, the internet and web design, handle the finances and all other details. A small manufacturer in Louisiana makes them, from fabric she buys in Dallas, or the garment district of Manhattan.

She says she knew nothing about e-commerce when she went into the project, but has never stopped learning.

In March she sold 250 of her bags, and in the summer she had orders for 400 more, priced between $80 and $170 dollars.

She had fall and winter lines ready to go to the makers in July 2000, and she was thinking about taking lessons in e-commerce.

That's Monica's story.

http://www.therealmonica.com

the ecademy ltd

The Ecademy Ltd is an education, training and consultancy network established in early 1999. It is based in London, but its community of members is worldwide, located in some 56 countries in both hemispheres.

At the heart of The Ecademy structure are the 'Twelve Principles of E-business,' developed after four years of interviews with, mixing with, and learning from some of the leading international figures in the internet world. The 'Principles' cover every aspect of business establishment, incorporating traditional approaches to business, and their integration into the electronic age.

For the sake of clarity, The Ecademy adopted the logo of a pizza, with each slice representing one of the 'Principles', making it easy for businesses to understand which parts come under the jurisdiction of which internal management sector.

The Ecademy is an advocate, and a dedicated user, of the community theme and its continual emphasis is on the imperative that lies behind a business establishing a community of customers and business partners in the electronic environment.

index